AS MY OWN SOUL

Other books by Chris Glaser:

Uncommon Calling
A Gay Christian's Struggle to Serve the Church

Come Home!
Reclaiming Spirituality and Community as Gay Men and Lesbians

Coming Out to God
Prayers for Lesbians and Gay Men, Their Families and Friends

The Word Is Out
Daily Reflections on the Bible for Lesbians and Gay Men

Coming Out as Sacrament

Reformation of the Heart
Seasonal Meditations by a Gay Christian

Unleashed
The Wit and Wisdom of Calvin the Dog

Communion of Life
Meditations for the New Millennium

Henri's Mantle
100 Meditations on Nouwen's Legacy

Troy Perry
Pastor and Prophet

AS MY OWN SOUL

The Blessing of Same-Gender Marriage

Chris Glaser

Seabury Books
NEW YORK

Copyright © 2009 by Chris R. Glaser

Unless otherwise noted, the Scripture quotations contained herein are from
the New Revised Standard Version Bible, copyright © 1989 by the Division
of Christian Education of the National Council of Churches of Christ in the
U.S.A. Used by permission. All rights reserved.

Cover design by Jennifer Glosser
Interior design and layout by MediaLynx Group, Inc.

Library of Congress Cataloging-in-Publication Data

Glaser, Chris.
    As my own soul : the blessing of same-gender marriage / Chris Glaser.
        p. cm.
    Includes bibliographical references.
    ISBN 978-1-59627-118-0 (pbk.)
    1. Same-sex marriage–Religious aspects–Christianity. I. Title.
    BT706.7.G63 2009
    261.8'3581–dc22
                                    2009016935

Seabury Books
445 Fifth Avenue
New York, New York 10016

www.seaburybooks.com

An imprint of Church Publishing Incorporated

5 4 3 2 1

*And it came to pass . . . that the soul of Jonathan was knit with
the soul of David, and Jonathan loved him
as his own soul.*
1 Samuel 18:1 (King James Version)

In thanksgiving to God for
John Boswell

Contents

Introduction

This book is written for those who want to understand more of what the debate around homosexuality and same-gender marriage is about within the Western Christian tradition in biblical, historical, cultural, and spiritual terms. It is intended for general readers, some of whom might be led to more detailed study in the books referenced and included in the bibliography. For some, this book will be covering familiar ground, but I hope from a fresh perspective, with different twists and emphases than other writings on the subject.

It is my opinion that the public debate on same-gender marriage has proven a blessing for the institution of marriage itself, just as the public debate on homosexuality has served as a blessing for the understanding of human sexuality. And for Christians, such conversations may help each of us discern and disclose not only our own views on marriage and human sexuality, but also our own ways of reading the Bible, encountering God, and following Jesus, guided by the Spirit, within the context of our faith and faith tradition.

May this book help all of us to look more deeply within ourselves and within marriage as well as within the mysteries of sexuality and companionship.

The Rev. Chris Glaser
Atlanta, Georgia

Acknowledgments

Thanks be to God that we live in a time when dialogue on same-gender marriage is possible! And that we may do so in the Body of Christ, the church!

And thanks be to God for the lesbian, gay, bisexual, and transgender community that has been an extended family for me!

Thanks to publisher Davis Perkins and editor Susan Erdey and others at Church Publishing for believing in this book, and to Susan for serving as an encouraging and helpful editor.

I am grateful for the scholarship of all whose work has shaped my thinking and graced this book, but in particular I wish to thank John Boswell, Bernadette Brooten, Stephanie Coontz, Bill Countryman, Marvin Ellison, Margaret Farley, Daniel Helminiak, Carter Heyward, Mary Hunt, James B. Nelson, Henri Nouwen, Jonathan Rauch, Jack Rogers, and John Witte, Jr.

My greatest inspiration for all of my writings have been the writers of the Bible and especially Jesus, who never wrote a thing, but whose life and sayings model for me inclusive compassion and spiritual maturity.

Thanks to cover designer Jennifer Glosser, book designer MediaLynx Group, Inc., and proofreader Gabriella Page-Fort for making this book all it could be. Thanks to all who market, distribute, and sell this book. All of these are the unsung heroes of the publishing business.

I thank my family—Wade Jones, our dog, Hobbes, and our late dog, Calvin—for their love and care of me.

And thanks to you, the reader, for joining me in this conversation on the blessing of same-gender marriage for all of us. May the conversation on marriage bless us all.

C.R.G

CHAPTER ONE

Claiming the Blessing

"I will not let you go unless you bless me."
— Genesis 32:26

The Present Moment

While writing this book in the fall of 2008 I attended a wedding in California of two longtime friends, George Lynch and Louie Tamantini. Thirty years ago George was "outed" on his way to ordination after seminary, but has continued to serve the church as a volunteer in a lay capacity with a denominational peacemaking program. Louie was reared Roman Catholic. They have lived together for fifteen years. Both attend West Hollywood Presbyterian Church, where I once served on staff, and their pastor, the Rev. Dan Smith, officiated at the ceremony. Family and friends gathered on a glorious day at their home for a brief ceremony in which they exchanged vows and rings. There were few dry eyes in the house.

When my partner and I had made our plans to fly from our home in Atlanta to attend, I realized it would occur the week of our own anniversary, celebrating eight years together. I noted also that the wedding happened to coincide with National Coming Out Day (October 11) and would be the day following the tenth anniversary of Matthew Shepard's brutal murder in Wyoming. During the ceremony the pastor reminded us of this synchronicity, as well as the ongoing struggle in California to retain this right at the ballot box the following month. The blessing of same-gender marriage had not come at the hands of the church but as a ruling from a primarily Republican-appointed California State Supreme Court. Little did we know at the time that a few weeks later, a state that would overwhelmingly help elect the progressive Democrat Barack Obama as president would also approve a ban on same-gender marriages by a 52% majority.

The week prior to the wedding I attended a friend's trial in Pittsburgh Presbytery for officiating at the wedding of Nancy McConn and Brenda Cole. The Rev. Janet Edwards is the descendent of famed eighteenth-century American preacher Jonathan Edwards. Janet and I became friends when we lived in the same dormitory at Yale Divinity School in the 1970s. I knew what a deliberate person she was; she rarely took any action without thinking it through with great care, considering what it would mean to the church, the community, the people, and the vocation she felt called to serve. Now, as she faced accusers who did not have the decency or courage to show their faces, she chose to invite friends and supporters from around the country to attend the trial to be held in the Grand Hall of the Priory, a name I considered worthy of the ecclesiastical intrigue of *The Da Vinci Code*! After the presentation of the cases and witnesses of the prosecution and the defense, as we awaited the verdict of the next morning, she invited everyone—opponents and supporters—for dinner and worship in a banquet hall at the Soldiers and Sailors Museum. Our seminary classmate, the Rev. Gail Ransom, led a creative worship, using innovative and interactive principles developed by Creation Spirituality theologian Matthew Fox. And I was to preach—an honor of great significance to me and to many in the room who knew of my nearly forty-year struggle as an activist within the church.

But what a tough text Janet asked me to preach on! The marriage feast of the Lamb, described in Revelation 19:5–10. This is the beatific vision of the future wedding of Jesus (the Lamb) with the faithful "'clothed with fine linen, bright and pure,'—for the fine linen is the righteous deeds of the saints" (Revelation 19:8). This is of course the *only* marriage truly "made in heaven." In fact, Jesus had declared there was no such thing as marriage in heaven when asked about resurrection (Mark 12:25). Yet the metaphor of Christ the groom and his Church as the bride is the basis for the later sacramentalization of marriage itself.

In this moment of conflict, Janet wanted to give everyone—including those who opposed her—a taste of the marriage feast of the Lamb. The theme of the evening was "A Time to Embrace: Toward Love and Reconciliation." In the sermon I described how many if not most of us knew what it meant to be prevented from embracing because of color, gender, disability, age, ethnicity, sexual orientation, or gender identity. Artificial barriers get in the way of what we really want. I explained,

> And what we want can be simply put: we want to belong. We want to belong to each other in marriage. We want to belong to our congregations in ministry. We want to belong to our vocations in service. And we want everyone to belong, even those whose privilege grants them immediate access to blessings we can only pray for, work for, struggle for, and sometimes die for. We have something to teach about gratitude for blessings too many take for granted.[1]

I also spoke of my recent experiences serving as interim pastor of several congregations and of my need to talk with those in conflict about *diabolos*, the New Testament word for *devil*, which literally means "divider" or "adversary." The spirit of division or divisiveness is what we experience as demonic. And the word to challenge division is *dialogue*, which literally means "through the word" and suggests finding common ground through what interim ministry training terms "holy conversations."[2]

As we engage in dialogue, we overcome the demonic within and among us, that adversarial spirit that would separate us from one another. I believe this may be applied not only to conflict within a particular congregation but disagreements within denominations and religious traditions. It is my hope that this book may further our holy conversations about marriage, and same-gender marriage in particular.

The proximity of the sermon to Saint Francis's feast day prompted me to recount how, in Nikos Kazantzakis's novel *Saint Francis*, the saint tells the narrator, Brother Leo, that even the Tempter, the devil, will enter paradise and be transformed. "How do you know, Brother Francis?" asks

Brother Leo. Saint Francis replies, "I know because of my heart, which opens and receives everything. Surely paradise must be the same."[3]

Now that's a vision worthy of Jesus. If even the devil may be reconciled, how much easier will it be for the adversaries around any particular conflict in the church!

The next morning the verdict was reached in *Pittsburgh Presbytery v. The Rev. Janet Edwards, Ph.D.* Because the Presbyterian Church (U.S.A.) does not recognize same-gender marriage, the court decided, it was not possible for Rev. Edwards to have performed a same-gender wedding, thus she did nothing, right or wrong!

"Where there is no vision the people perish," Proverbs 29:18 (KJV) declares. What Janet Edwards offered as a vision, the church declared an apparition.

Another of our friends who lived in Bushnell House, our dorm at Yale Divinity School, was Barbara Brown Taylor. In her book *Leaving Church* and recent interviews, she grieves how conflicts like the one over homosexuality have surfaced dogmatic litmus tests for Episcopalians. She observes that the Anglican Church she loved was not so much a church of common beliefs as it was a church of common prayer. Scholars such as Elaine Pagels in *Beyond Belief* have documented how diverse beliefs characterized the church from its onset. And during Janet's trial, one of her defense witnesses, Dr. Chris Elrod of Louisville Presbyterian Theological Seminary, had quoted John Calvin to the effect that no one person can discern the truth—that's why we need to keep speaking to one another.

The Social Context

"Marriage gives you more authenticity, more equality," declared Cody Rogahn after marrying his partner, Jonathan Yarborough, in Provincetown, Massachusetts. "It gives you the same things heterosexuals have, and everybody should have, if they want to be in a committed relationship with another person." The couple, already together eight years, were among the first to apply for a marriage license the day it became legal in the state, May 17, 2004—the fiftieth anniversary of the U.S. Supreme Court striking down the concept of "separate but equal" in *Brown v. Board of Education*. On the same day, then President George W. Bush called once again for a Constitutional amendment to ban same-sex marriage, and six states prepared to vote later that year on similar amendments to state constitutions: Georgia, Kentucky, Mississippi, Missouri, Oklahoma, and Utah.[4]

On that day, Massachusetts joined Belgium, the Netherlands, and three Canadian provinces in legally marrying gay couples. Canada since has recognized same-gender marriage nationwide, as have Norway, Spain, and Sweden. Connecticut's Supreme Court legalized same-gender marriage in November 2008. Vermont earlier had led the way in recognizing civil unions, and in April 2009 passed legislation allowing same gender marriage; the governor vetoed the legislation; and the legislature overrode the governor's veto on April 7, 2009. That same day, the Washington, DC, council voted to recognize same-sex marriages performed in other states, joining New York State. The Iowa Supreme Court declared that state's anti-same-gender marriage amendment unconstitutional on April 3, 2009. Maine's legislation passed and its governor signed a same-gender marriage bill on May 7, 2009.

Many municipalities have registries for domestic partners, and an increasing number of businesses provide domestic partner benefits—all of which cultural observer Jonathan Rauch refers to as "marriage lite." He has noted that it is these less-than-equal unions that actually weaken the institution of marriage, not same-gender marriage, because many heterosexual couples have opted for these lesser alternatives rather than embrace marriage itself.[5] He believes if marriage were valued as a universal good for gays and straights alike, the institution of marriage would benefit, much as extending the vote to blacks and women strengthened that franchise and American democracy.

Back in 2004, in other areas of the United States, such as San Francisco, upstate New York, and counties in Oregon and Colorado, marriage certificates were granted to same-gender couples until higher authorities intervened. The pleasant spectacle of gay and lesbian couples standing in line for hours and sometimes days to marry indicates, at least to some, that marriage is alive and well in the United States. Witnessing these news events on television stirred support from people previously indifferent to same-gender marriage, ranging from the late Prince Sihanouk of Cambodia, who declared his country should have it, to a self-described "regular guy" who wrote of his changed mind in a letter to the editor in a Southern newspaper.

Of course, it also stirred negative reactions, especially from the religious right, led by the late Jerry Falwell, Pat Robertson, James Dobson, Lou Sheldon, and others who viewed the advancement of gay people in society as a sign of cultural decadence and the nation's imminent moral downfall. Marriage and family are believed by some Americans to be under attack, and often their objections are based in religion. But there is no neat conservative–liberal political dichotomy on the issue: some conservative voices have also been raised in support of same-gender marriage, or at least equitable rights. Journalist Anna Quindlen observed the conservative and progressive nature of same-gender marriage: "Same-gender marriage is a radical notion for straight people and a conservative notion for gay ones."[6]

What has fueled the furor over gay rights and marriage was the essential legalization of sex between consenting adults of the same gender in private by the U.S. Supreme Court striking down state sodomy laws in 2003, and the subsequent Massachusetts and California Supreme Courts rulings requiring those states to give marital rights to same-gender couples, finding no prevailing governmental or societal interest in excluding homosexual citizens from those rights. These rulings could both be interpreted as *conservative* decisions, saving citizens from undue governmental intrusion in private matters in the first case, and preventing legislative or popular vote trampling on individual rights in the second. But those who oppose both decisions think marriage must be saved from "activist" judges, though most federal judges presently on the bench have been appointed by Republican administrations, and the same U.S. Supreme Court that struck down antigay laws also found in favor of a Republican president in a disputed election.

John Witte, Jr., director of the Law and Religion Program at Atlanta's Emory University, introduces his exhaustive academic tome on marriage in this way:

> Oliver Wendell Holmes, Jr., once said that all the great questions of theology and philosophy must ultimately come to the

law for their resolution. Holmes's claim, while overstated, has merit for this book. While theologians and philosophers have debated questions of the origin, nature, and purpose of marriage, jurists and judges have had to resolve them—in general statutes as well as in concrete cases. Such legal formulations have invariably reflected, and sometimes reified, prevailing theological ideas and ideals respecting marriage.[7]

The Religious Context

Forty years ago, religious bodies and the broader society began grappling with homosexuality and homosexual persons, whose emergence as a much more visible community in the United States began after World War II and as a political influence after the sexual revolution of the 1960s. Roman Catholics began to question Vatican pronouncements on human sexuality, including what the Vatican called the "intrinsic disorder" of homosexuality. Protestants began wrestling with the issue of homosexuality by addressing the question of the ordination of self-acknowledged gays and lesbians who expressed their sexuality in responsible ways, including covenant relationships. Some Christians noted that the church needed first to address the issue of same-gender marriage if the church was to hold all of its leadership accountable to the same standards of fidelity and chastity. They felt we were putting the cart before the horse discussing ordination of gay and lesbian individuals prior to the ordering of gay and lesbian relationships. So, as precipitous as the same-gender marriage debate has been portrayed, our current dialogue on the subject is, in truth, long overdue.

In the public square, it may be that the wrangling on same-gender marriage has proven a blessing for the institution of marriage itself, just as the debate on homosexuality has served as a blessing for the understanding of human sexuality. In the religious sector, though we may not like conflict within our ranks and fear loss of members and even schism, it could be said—some would say too optimistically—that our wrestling with these issues has *benefited* religious bodies as well. For Christians, such wrestling serves as an occasion to discern and disclose not only our own views on marriage and human sexuality, but also our own ways of reading the Bible, encountering God, and following Jesus, guided by the Spirit, within the context of our faith and faith tradition. The dialogue isn't the problem—it's the contentious way we often do the dialogue or resist the dialogue that may diminish our spirits and reject the Holy Spirit.

"All things work together for good for those who love God and are called according to God's purpose," the apostle Paul affirmed.[8] This doesn't mean those who love God and are called to serve don't suffer, experience discomfort, and endure conflict, as the apostle indicates earlier in Romans. Rather, it means that faithful people will find God and the good in every circumstance.

The Old Testament figure Jacob is said to have wrestled with God.[9] It was a hands-on, intimate struggle in the night. And Jacob demanded a blessing. To our ears, grappling with God seems unthinkable. Placing our hand on the awesome Lord of the universe seems implausible. And demanding a blessing—from anyone, let alone the Creator of all that is—seems impertinent. Isn't the very nature of blessing God's grace—unmerited, unearned favor? Yet Jacob was given his blessing and renamed Israel, "one who strives with God." Despite God's blessing, perhaps rather *because* of God's blessing, Jacob had yet to reconcile with his brother Esau, who perceived Jacob as stealing his birthright.

Throughout the scriptures, we see people of faith striving with God: bargaining, negotiating, pleading, seeking signs, asking forgiveness, claiming blessings—from the Garden of Eden to the garden of Gethsemane. Our Lord himself asked that God deliver him from the cup he was about to drink, the suffering he was to endure. In the midst of that suffering on the cross, he cried out to know why God abandoned him, yet he gave up his spirit to God's will and God's care. His trust in God led from the garden of Gethsemane to the garden of the empty tomb.

Though many of our theologies have since constructed a less pliable God, the truth is that we still contend with God. We still plead and bargain and claim blessings. I suspect it's something about being human, an imprint of Eden when God wrestled clay into human form for companionship, and took walks with us in the cool of the day. For

Christians, the communion of that innocent time is tasted again in the bread and wine we share with One who wrestled into human flesh out of love for us. Yet Communion is also a foretaste of the communion to come, the marriage feast of the Lamb, the kingdom or commonwealth of God that is in-breaking even now, transforming our old ways of understanding and living in the world.

We all struggle with God: people of all colors and abilities and ages and genders and sexualities. We also wrestle with "the powers that be" on this earth. We claim the blessings endowed every human being: equal opportunities, equal rights, equal privileges, equal responsibilities. Socially, marriage is a privilege. Legally, marriage is a right. Spiritually, marriage is a calling, a vocation. In all three categories, marriage is a responsibility. Recently, lesbians and gay men are claiming this blessing and its responsibilities for themselves, socially, legally, and spiritually. Yet there is resistance. Social resistance. Legal resistance. Religious resistance. Paradoxically, some who denied gay and lesbian people other blessings because they were believed incapable of forming long-term exclusive relationships now resist them claiming the blessing of marriage. And yet, in the United States, the majority of citizens, while not necessarily affirming homosexuality or same-gender marriage, believe lesbian and gay couples should be afforded some form of legal rights and protections.[10]

Lesbians and gay men of faith have struggled with God, grappled to understand their sexuality in the context of their faith, wrestled for God's blessings in their relationships. Despite God's blessing, perhaps rather *because* of God's blessing, gays and lesbians feel called to reconcile with heterosexual brothers and sisters, some of whom may perceive them as "stealing" their birthright of marriage.

Church and culture may come to realize that the struggle is about something deeper than homosexuality or homosexual persons. The travail is over something essentially human and holy, the *imago dei* within each one of us that calls us to coupling, communion, and community. That's the blessing of the same-gender marriage debate: it helps us look deeply within ourselves and within the institution of marriage and the mysteries of human sexuality, spirituality, and companionship.

Claiming the Blessing of Marriage

There is some difference of interpretation over whether Jacob contended with God or with an angel of the Lord. But such messengers of the Lord served as God's presence to those to whom they appeared. Today individual Christians wrestle with God's messenger the church; in other words, with one another. Rather than regret the struggle, as we often do, we do better to realize that this is a human condition as well as the Christian dynamic: to wrestle with our conscience and the consciences of our sister and brother Christians, respecting that "God alone is Lord of the conscience."[11] Christian tradition—the Bible, creeds and confessions, literature and history—invites us to grapple too with our spiritual ancestors, guided by the Spirit. And we must also face the church of the future, being faithful in this time and place so that our posterity may be blessed by our legacy.

The peace which we seek in the church is not necessarily the absence of struggle. Though uncertain, it is believed the Greek word for peace, *eirene*, comes from the root *eiro*, "to fasten together." As the writer of Ephesians described Gentile and Jewish Christians blended in the same church despite their cultural and philosophical differences, "Christ is our peace." Jesus Christ is what binds us together as Christians.

Throughout this book, scripture will play a central role, and the texts that are the "usual suspects" will be discussed. If the issue were readily settled by the Bible, however, Christians would not hold such divergent opinions, as can be seen by the wide spectrum of Christian positions and scholarly interpretations on homosexuality and the Bible. Respected scholars such as Johanna Bos, Walter Brueggemann, Victor Paul Furnish, Peter Gomes, Carter Heyward, Robin Scroggs, Jeffrey Siker, Helmut Thielicke, Walter Wink, and others have concluded, in Siker's words, "the Bible has relatively little to say that directly informs us about how to address the issue of homosexual Christians today. The Bible certainly does not positively condone homosexuality as a legitimate expression of human sexuality, but neither does it expressly exclude loving monogamous homosexual adult Christian relationships from being within the realm of God's intentions for humanity."[12]

The declaration that "the Bible says what it means and means what it says" gives short shrift to the multilayered intentions of its writers and the complexities of their cultures and eras and circumstances, as well as to the Holy Spirit, who, through the ages, has led succeeding generations of Christians into "further truth," as Jesus promised. The "plain meaning" of scripture also fails to account for our own bias and possible ignorance in approaching the Bible. It could be said that such a method for reading the Bible does not take the authority of the Bible seriously enough. Reading the Bible requires first "reading" *ourselves*, both what we bring to the text and what we cannot bring to the text without scholarly help. It invites comparisons within the Bible itself. And, ultimately, reading the words of scripture must take us deeper—to God's ultimate revelation for Christians, the Word of God, Jesus Christ.

Other Times the Church Changed Its Mind

Same-gender marriage is the occasion to be faithful in our own time. While race and gender and abortion are still matters of conflict, they were even more so at various times in church history, and are still volatile in various venues of Christian faith (such as Eastern Orthodox or Roman Catholic attitudes toward women as priests and Southern Baptist rejection of women as lead pastors). Many Christians hold that the stakes are higher today because they believe that gay and lesbian acceptance challenges biblical authority, Christian sexual ethics, church boundaries, and the institution of marriage. Yet this was also the perception of past controversies. Slavery and segregation, as well as the subjugation of women, were justified with scripture. Women's suffrage, women's ordination, equality in marriage, and a woman's right to make decisions about her own body were viewed (and still are viewed in some circles) as a rejection of traditional sexual ethics and family values, as well as destructive of the institutions of church and marriage and family.

We may not remember (or even know) the anguish of past conflict, just as the mother whom Jesus describes "no longer remembers the anguish [of childbirth] because of the joy." With this metaphor, Jesus comforted his disciples who were about to suffer his loss (John 16:20–21).

The New Testament devotes many pages to arguably the greatest and most controversial experience in church history, when the Gentiles were "grafted onto the root of Jesse" without first converting to Judaism. We are so focused on our present time that we cannot grasp the revulsion that Jews felt for immoral, illegal (because they did not follow the Law of Moses), and unclean Gentiles. The controversy of accepting them "as they are" is arguably the single greatest conflict of the early church, described and addressed in various ways throughout Christian scripture. And yet that's just what the church did, accept them as they were. Jewish Christians had to overcome their visceral reactions and religious scruples and Gentile Christians and their advocates had to be mindful of Christians of "weaker" consciences. So there is precedent, and the church was able to be evangelical, proclaiming the gospel to the ends of the earth as Jesus commanded, when it chose to be inclusive.

As a denomination in the mainstream, Presbyterians may serve as a case study of how the churches in America changed their minds on earlier controversial issues and help us see the parallel with the present conflict. I believe it only fair to consider the beam in the eye of my own denomination. The Rev. Jack Rogers, professor of theology *emeritus* at San Francisco Theological Seminary and former Moderator of the Presbyterian Church (U.S.A.), has documented how Presbyterians changed their minds and thus became "more faithful to the intent of the biblical and confessional writers"[13] in an insightful and practical book, *Reading the Bible and the Confessions*. Though specifically Presbyterian, the cases have parallels in other ecclesiastical settings. And though religious, these shifts in interpretation of the Bible and church tradition have parallels in the changing constitutional and legal interpretations of the civil sphere. Indeed, the changes often occurred in tandem. Rogers reminds us, "Cultures are relative and should never be treated as rigid and timeless expressions of God's will."[14]

I have selected those changes having to do with race, women, and marriage. The parallels I draw with the present controversy of homosexuality and same-gender marriage are my own.

We Changed Our Minds on Race

In the early 1800s, Presbyterian theologians justified slavery because no particular text in the Bible directly opposed it.[15] No particular text in the Bible directly affirms homosexuality and same-gender marriage. Yet just as broader biblical themes led people of faith to question and challenge slavery, so they may lead us to question and challenge as well as shape our positions on homosexuality and same-gender marriage.

Though an 1818 General Assembly spoke of the evils of slavery, it used "[the slaves'] ignorance, and their vicious habits generally" to refrain from endorsing abolition. In 1861, Presbyterians split north and south over the issue of slavery, and the Presbyterian Church of the Confederate States of America justified slavery: "As long as that race, in its comparative degradation co-exists, side by side, with the white, bondage is its normal condition."[16] Thus slavery was justified by the *lifestyles* of African-Americans in captivity, with all its attendant social ills. Today there are references to "the homosexual lifestyle," as if all gay men and lesbians adhered to a single lifestyle, rather than representing the same diversity of life patterns embraced by heterosexuals. The "lifestyle" may be associated with a particular segment of the gay community, as imprecise a judgment as associating the straight community with, to take an example, those who frequent singles bars rather than enter into marriage. In either case, that of African-Americans or gay and lesbian Americans, to make a case for enslavement or exclusion based on conditions *created by* enslavement or exclusion would seem unfair and prejudicial.

On behalf of the new Confederate denomination, a theologian declared, "Whatever is universal is natural. We are willing that slavery should be tried by this standard."[17] Because slavery was commonly practiced, historically and cross-culturally, it was considered "natural." The common practice of heterosexual marriage historically and cross-culturally also argues for it being "natural" for all. We may concede it being the norm at the same time realizing it may not be natural for those with a homosexual orientation, no more than slavery would be considered "natural" by the slaves themselves. We may compare it to patriarchy, which has been nearly universally practiced, or to men having multiple wives, which was permitted in 980 of 1,154 past or present societies for which there is an anthropological record.[18]

In 1867, the most prominent southern Presbyterian theologian in the latter half of the nineteenth century, citing biblical texts describing but not condemning slavery, "argued against the ordination of African Americans . . . with these words: 'Every hope of the existence of church and state, and of civilization itself, hangs upon our arduous effort to defeat the doctrine of Negro suffrage.' And more than twenty years later, in 1888, he wrote that 'the radical social theory' that asserts 'all men are born free and equal' was an 'attack upon God's Word.'"[19] In retrospect, we can see how both of these statements overdramatize the effect of change. Indeed, we may even come to the conclusion that had change not been effected, these dire results—the decline of civilization, the attack on God's Word—would have been more nearly realized. Conservative columnist Maggie Gallagher has offered a similarly hysterical analysis of same-gender marriage, "We are poised to lose the gay-marriage battle badly. It means losing the marriage debate. It means losing limited government. It means losing American civilization."[20] Yet what would be lost if *more* people married rather than fewer? Would anyone's marriage end or be diminished by allowing same-gender marriage?

In 1954, southern Presbyterians adopted desegregation ten days after the U.S. Supreme Court essentially ruled the same in *Brown v. Board of Education*.[21] Despite coming afterward, the southern denomination nonetheless acted prophetically because most of the South would resist the court's decision. What the court adjudicated on constitutional grounds, the church adjudicated on biblical and confessional standards. The church did not follow the culture, but found its own way to the same conclusion, even at risk of alienating its primary mission field. There is no ruling yet on same-gender marriage from the U.S. Supreme Court, though it did decline to hear an appeal of the Massachusetts' Supreme Court decision, which had said, in part, "The marriage ban works a deep and scarring hardship on a very real segment of the community for no rational reason. . . . We construe civil marriage to mean the voluntary union of two persons as spouses, to the exclusion of all others." The states have regulated marriage with two notable exceptions, when the U.S. Supreme Court struck down polygamy in Utah and later struck down laws against interracial marriage in seventeen states. Affecting fewer people, the court also found in favor of a prisoner marrying without a warden's consent. As with desegregation, if and when the church decides to bless same-gender marriages, it will do so independently and for its own reasons. Whether or not the church will prove prophetic in this area remains to be seen.

We Changed Our Minds on Women

Women's contributions to the church were considered initially "ornamental" rather than substantive.[22] This is roughly the same as the welcome most denominations offer lesbian, gay, bisexual, and transgender people (often abbreviated LGBT people), while largely denying them opportunities for service, leadership, ministry, and marriage. Ministry may be offered to LGBT people and their families to varying extents if at all, and the church receives their money, talents, and time. Yet without access to positions of authority, openly LGBT people do not have as much opportunity to substantively affect or shape the nature, mission, and ministry of the church as a whole. Women got around their own church disenfranchisement in the past by sheer numbers and their wholehearted engagement with the church at various levels; LGBT members have, to some extent, been able to do the same—not by sheer numbers, but by their wholehearted engagement.

The primary northern Presbyterian theologian of the nineteenth century critically reviewed a book against slavery by using "the analogy of the necessary subordination of women. He wrote, 'If women are to be emancipated from subjection to the law which God has imposed upon them, . . . [i]f in studied insult to the authority of God, we are to renounce, in the marriage contract, all claim to obedience, . . . there is no deformity of human character from which we turn with deeper loathing than from a woman forgetful of her nature and clamorous for the vocations and rights of men.'"[23] Readers will have heard phrases such as this applied to lesbian and gay couples claiming their blessings: "insult to the authority of God," "deformity of human character," "loathing [for one] forgetful of [her or his] nature," "clamorous for the vocations and rights" of heterosexuals. And the ideal of marriage assumed in this statement includes "the necessary subordination [and obedience] of women."

When the 1916 General Assembly of southern Presbyterians reaffirmed the denomination's ban on women preaching and being ordained, it nonetheless allowed women to speak at mixed gatherings (of women and men) such as congregational prayer meetings at the discretion of the session (church council) of the particular church. Sixty-one commissioners (delegates) protested this as a violation of biblical authority![24] Presbyterians would subsequently endorse the ordination of women as elders and deacons, and twenty-five years after that support the ordination of women as ministers. By the time of a case that came before the highest church court in 1974, in which a candidate for ordination opposed the ordination of women, the jurists declared of women's equality in church service, "It is evident from our Church's confessional standards that the Church believes the Spirit of God has led us into new understandings of this equality before God."[25] This shift from viewing the leadership of women as "a violation of Biblical authority" to "the Spirit of God" leading them "into new understandings of [their] equality" took generations and, in practice, is yet to be fully appreciated and manifest in the church. Though changes as great as this may be accelerated in our own era by means of expanded and more timely access to education, information, and experience, the history of women in the church attests both the need of endurance and openness to the Spirit in terms of the present issues. Will our posterity, the church of the future, be as surprised by our own attitudes toward lesbians and gay men and same-gender marriage as we are at those of our spiritual forebears in relation to women? Polls of young voters indicate they already are.

We Changed Our Minds about Marriage

Presbyterians inherited Puritan attitudes toward marriage, reflected in the earliest version of the Westminster Catechism, which declared adherents should "marry onely in the Lord" and not "marry with infidels, papists or other idolaters," referring to the pope as the Anti-Christ! In reaction to Roman Catholic celibacy, marriage was essentially required, and "undue delay of marriage" was a sin. Marriages were arranged by parents, a practice affirmed by the Second Helvetic Confession. The primary purpose of marriage was children. But, in the 1930s, American Presbyterians resisted the ban on marriage with Catholics, conceding, rather patronizingly, "many Roman Catholics are sincere and intelligent believers in our Lord Jesus Christ." The Westminster Confession was amended to remove negative references to the pope and the prohibition of marriage with Roman Catholics.[26]

When the Federal Council of Churches advised parents to consider birth control in 1931, the southern Presbyterians withdrew and the northern Presbyterians admonished that the ecumenical body "should hold its peace on questions of delicacy and morality." By 1960, the two denominations issued a joint statement approving birth control, based on a shift in Presbyterian attitudes as to the purpose of marriage. Marriage was now believed to serve the personal fulfillment of the couple rather than the goal of propagation. In turn, this change of heart allowed a more thoughtful consideration of divorce.[27] Readers can see how it would also allow a more compassionate consideration of same-gender marriage.

Yet more parallel is the way slave marriages were viewed. The dominant white culture did not recognize slave marriages. Couples could be bought and sold separately. Nonetheless, slaves devised rituals to celebrate their commitments, rituals gradually recognized by the church, especially Presbyterians. Hanover Presbytery in 1791 determined that cohabiting slaves could be considered married "in the sight of God" and by the "mutual consent of the Parties." Divorce and remarriage was possible for slaves sold separately from one another, because each partner of the separated couple could remarry as if "the other were dead" and still be church members. A similar "as if dead" notion came to be applied to adultery and abandonment in later Presbyterian considerations of divorce and remarriage. As a result, a 1930 northern Presbyterian study allowed remarriage for the partner abandoned through infidelity or desertion, concluding "Anything that kills love and deals death to the spirit of the union is infidelity," citing 2 Corinthians 3:6, "The letter killeth; but the spirit giveth life" (KJV). A 1950 southern Presbyterian council, while not recommending changes to church policy on marriage and divorce, nonetheless decried the use of proof-texts in the matter, as such texts had more than one interpretation and failed to take into account Jesus' full teachings. Both north and south agreed to change the Westminster Confession's teaching on divorce and remarriage in the 1950s, affirming the first duty of marriage was to the couple involved, not society. Rogers concludes,

> Whereas it took over a century for the church to cope with entrenched injustices to African Americans and women, the church changed its stance on the matter of divorce and remarriage in thirty-three years, between 1926 and 1959. Might it be that one significant difference was that those present and voting in presbyteries and General Assembly were vulnerable to divorce and thus could feel the necessity for change? Regarding racial injustice or women's equality, however, because those voting in presbyteries were all white and all men, they were able to distance themselves from those affected by their decisions. They could treat the problems "objectively" and focus on the good of society in general. But when it touched them, as with all human beings, their concerns become much more personal and pastoral.[28]

Clearly, the same dynamic is at work in denominations that do not permit openly LGBT people to participate in legislative counsels of the church. Proof-texting as an inadequate way of discerning God's will or Jesus' full teaching is also applicable in the treatment of LGBT Christians who are all too familiar with the handful of so-called "clobber passages" employed by those who seem all too unfamiliar with the numerous passages about God's grace and freedom in Jesus Christ. The new understanding of the purpose of marriage as the personal fulfillment of the couple supports the consideration of same-gender marriage. And, just as Christians were among the first to grant some recognition to slave marriages when illegal, Christians have been among the first to recognize same-gender marriages even when not legally sanctioned.

In the changing attitudes toward race, women, and marriage, the Presbyterian Church serves as an example of shifts occurring in many Christian traditions in recent centuries. In liberation theology there is said to be among God's people a "memory of the future," which means that God's liberating presence in the past reminds us of God's liberating presence in the future. Just as Christians of the past addressed other controversial issues in good faith, so we may believe that we will do the same as we consider same-gender marriage.

Banning the Inevitable

There has been a flurry of proposed and enacted state constitutional amendments or laws banning same-gender marriage, and presidents and members of Congress of both major parties have passed the Defense of Marriage Act or proposed an amendment to the U.S. Constitution. When governing bodies resort to codifying an institution exclusively for one class, such as ordination in the church or marriage in civil society, a sea change has already happened that requires building a wall against the tide. No wall will withstand the sea indefinitely, and so, such activity may be viewed as a sign of hope rather than a cause for despair.

Jonathan Rauch has expressed hope that a decision on same-gender marriage not come down from on high, either in the form of an amendment to the U.S. Constitution or a U.S. Supreme Court ruling. He prefers a Federalist approach, by which states such as Massachusetts or California or Vermont might try out same-gender marriage and demonstrate to other states its viability and value to society. A Supreme Court decision could foster a reactionary response that could be destructive to the country in general and to the LGBT community in particular. That could be said to be true of the *Brown v. Board of Education* case, after which, as example, some public school districts closed altogether rather than comply with desegregation, establishing private schools for white children.

A "local option" policy could work for the church as well, in which individual congregations by choice may bless same-gender marriages before a denominational policy is set in stone. This has earlier been suggested for the question of ordination. Eventually, however, at a time of greater consensus on the matter in either the church or the state, a uniform arrangement would best serve each. I would argue that *Brown v. Board of Education* did not happen prematurely, but at a time when it was both needed and yet was based on a growing consensus. To assist the building of consensus for same-gender marriage, it will help to consider sexuality taboos, the history of Western marriage, the association of marriage with the sacred, Jesus and sexuality, and the spirituality of marriage—especially as these concerns relate to same-gender marriage. These are the themes of the chapters that follow.

What we know already is that the culture and the church can each change its mind. The process may look like a "culture war," a slogan used by Nazis facing off with Jews, dissidents, gay men, Romas, and other minorities in the 1930s. But for society, it may simply be a cultural evolution that seems to move forward in fits and starts, yet retrospectively, flows in a natural but slow-moving process of adaptation to newly discovered realities.

For the church, the Spirit may simply be leading us into "further truth" so that we may do "greater things" as Jesus promised. In Christianity, believers have been encouraged to live proleptically by the apostle Paul, to live "as if" the kingdom or reign of God were already here. The reign of God is already among us, Jesus proclaimed, thus placing "the way things should be"—human custom—in a different light, an eternal perspective. The reign of God was understood as ushering in justice and peace. It could be said that many same-gender couples, along with several states and nations and many congregations, are following that spiritual counsel by establishing and recognizing same-gender marriages. We may trust that, as God has been there for us in the midst of change in the past, God continues to be with us, leading us by the open-heartedness of Christ.

Notes

[1] Chris Glaser, "A Marriage Made in Heaven," a sermon on the occasion of the trial of The Rev. Dr. Janet McCune Edwards, October 1, 2008, Pittsburgh, Pennsylvania.

[2] Gil Rendle and Alice Mann, *Holy Conversations: Strategic Planning as a Spiritual Practice for Congregations* (Bethesda, MD: The Alban Institute, 2003).

[3] Nikos Kazantzakis, *Saint Francis* (Chicago: Loyola Classics, 2005), 288–289.

[4] David Ho, "Couples Make History: Massachusetts is first state to permit same-sex weddings," *The Atlanta Journal-Constitution*, May 18, 2004, front page.

[5] Jonathan Rauch, *Gay Marriage: Why It Is Good for Gays, Good for Straights, and Good for America* (New York: Times Books, 2004), 6.

[6] Anna Quindlen, quoted by Christine Pierce, "Same-gender marriage," in *Same-Sex Marriage: The Moral and Legal Debate*, ed. Robert M. Baird and Stuart E. Rosenbaum (Amherst, NY: Prometheus Books, 1997), 171. Also quoted by Marvin Ellison, *Same-Sex Marriage? A Christian Ethical Analysis* (Cleveland: The Pilgrim Press, 2004), 119.

[7] John Witte, Jr., *From Sacrament to Contract: Marriage, Religion, and Law in the Western Tradition* (Louisville, KY: Westminster John Knox Press, 1997), 1.

[8] Romans 8:28.

[9] Genesis 32:22–32.

[10] *Newsweek* poll, detailed in "A Gay Marriage Surge: Public support grows, according to the new *Newsweek* Poll" (*www.newsweek.com,* December, 2008).

[11] The Form of Government, The Presbyterian Church (U.S.A.), Chapter I, Preliminary Principles, 3.The Historic Principles of Church Order, G-1.0301.

[12] Jeffrey S. Siker, "How to Decide? Homosexual Christians, the Bible, and Gentile Inclusion," *Theology Today*, Vol. 52, No. 2 (July 1994), 226.

[13] Jack Rogers, *Reading the Bible and the Confessions: The Presbyterian Way* (Louisville, KY: Geneva Press, 1999), 4.

[14] Rogers, 47.

[15] Rogers, 40.

[16] Rogers, 42.

[17] Rogers, 109.

[18] Rauch, 16. Referencing Robin Wright in *The Moral Animal: Why We Are the Way We Are: The New Science of Evolutionary Psychology* (New York: Pantheon, 1994).

[19] Rogers, 49.

[20] Rauch, 5.

[21] Rogers, 79.

[22] Rogers, 3.

[23] Rogers, 102–103.

[24] Rogers, 37.

[25] Rogers, 104.

[26] Rogers, 82, 84.

[27] Rogers, 115.

[28] Rogers, 116–121. Quoted conclusion is on page 121.

CHAPTER TWO

Deeper Than Scripture

Taboo, Shame and Sex-Negativity Biblical, Cultural, and Visceral Responses

*"Do not think that I have come to bring peace to the earth;
I have not come to bring peace, but a sword."*
— Jesus in Matthew 10:34 (NRSV)

Why are the issues of homosexuality and same-gender marriage so extraordinarily divisive and volatile in churches today? Why is the negative gut response to homosexuality so strong in so many people, including people of faith? Why are people rushing to defend marriage between a man and a woman as if it were under attack? What is the source of the panic, as if there are not enough marriage licenses to go around?

Long before the present controversy, the Rev. Eileen Lindner, a Presbyterian minister, once asked me questions like these. She has more than a passing knowledge of the church, then serving the National Council of Churches and holding a Ph.D. in American church history. Having worked on matters of race, women, and abortion, she has observed that the issue of homosexuality ignites passions the like of which she has not seen in these other arenas. This chapter is an attempt, not to completely answer such questions, but to put forward possible explanations. In the present storm of controversy, many Christians are like the disciples hounding the sleeping Jesus during a Galilean storm at sea to do something (see Mark 4:35–41). Why are we so anxious? What makes this conflict different from other recent storms?

When it comes to marriage and family, it must be noted that homosexuality and same-gender marriage are the divisions *du jour*. In his conclusion to his remarkable *From Sacrament to Marriage: Marriage, Religion, and Law in the Western Tradition*, cited earlier, John Witte, Jr. notes that "family crises on a comparable scale to those we face today have been faced before. And bitter jeremiads about the end of civil society and the dissolution of all social order have been voiced before— by Chrysostom and Augustine in the fifth century, by Aquinas and Hugh St. Victor in the thirteenth century, by Luther and Calvin in the sixteenth century."[1]

The Visceral: Taboo

What makes homosexuality and same-gender marriage gut-wrenching for many is not simply that they are believed to be unethical, or legislated by others as illegal. It is because homosexuality is taboo, a human custom virtually prerational, part of our cultural mores (thus morality). In my first book, *Uncommon Calling*, I described my sister guessing my carefully guarded secret: "You're a homosexual!" "How did you know?" I asked. "Oh," she said, surprised that she was correct, "if you were a maniac going around killing people, you could talk about that, even write a book about it! But no one can talk about homosexuality." She was accurate; homosexuality is more taboo than violence in our culture, evidenced by the violence that permeates everything from children's cartoons to the plethora of crime dramas on television and at the theater. In contrast, the first television drama about AIDS, *An Early Frost*, depicted little if any physical contact between the featured male couple—even as one lay dying from AIDS—out of fear of a hostile viewer reaction. In *Christianity, Social Tolerance and Homosexuality*, the late Yale historian John Boswell wrote that the homosexual taboo was second only to incest.

To support heterosexuals trying to understand their possibly negative feelings toward homosexuals, ranging from discomfort to repugnance,

I explain in my presentations that lesbians and gay men usually suffer similar antagonism toward our own feelings, though this is changing among younger generations. This is why some of the harshest attacks may come from individuals anxious about and repressing their own sexuality or from self-proclaimed "reformed" homosexuals, and why community-building among gays and lesbians is hampered by what most marginalized groups experience as "lateral violence," negativity directed "laterally" among members of the oppressed community rather than against oppressors. When combined with the rejecting attitudes of others, including churches, many LGBT people resort to self-destructive behavior or outright suicide, which in turn, is used as evidence of our pathology. Antipathy toward homosexuality is learned by all of us in a way that sexual orientation is not, according to contemporary researchers.[2]

This underlying feeling must be addressed in any discussion on same-gender marriage. We cannot value, let alone champion, an institution that embraces individuals or behaviors that at the least make us uncomfortable, and at the worst make us sick, sick to our stomachs or sick at heart. Let me give a somewhat comparable example. With the late activist pastor William Sloane Coffin, I am a recovering racist, sexist, and homophobe.[3] My racism was never explicit or boorish in its expressions. But, for example, I somehow "got" that mixed race marriage wasn't "the way things should be." This attitude did not come from my mind, it was ingrained in my gut, and I have no idea where or from whom I learned it. And though my attitudes changed, for a while I still carried a small, strange feeling inside of me when I saw a mixed race couple. If I let that feeling get the better (or the worse!) of me, I suppose I could have offered all kinds of "rational" explanations for my prejudice. But, if push came to shove, my underlying argument against mixed race marriage would have been simply, "Because that's not what I'm used to." In *Same Sex Marriage?*, ethicist Marvin Ellison explains that, historically, I was not alone:

> As early as 1705, a Massachusetts law was enacted to ban interracial coupling. By the end of the nineteenth century, at least forty states had similar laws forbidding people from marrying a spouse of the "wrong race." The California courts were the first

in the nation to declare an interracial marriage ban unconstitutional, but that ruling was handed down only in 1948. Because of the unfettered power of Jim Crow segregation at the time, the decision was widely denounced as threatening the stability of Western civilization. As one Southern judge argued, "Almighty God created the races, white, black, yellow, malay and red, and he placed them on separate continents. And but for the interference with his arrangement there would be no cause for such marriages. The fact that he separated the races shows that he did not intend for the races to mix."[4]

It took nearly twenty years for the U.S. Supreme Court to catch up to California in 1967's *Loving v. Virginia* decision, voiding similar bans and defining marriage among our "personal vital rights." Given the present turmoil over same-gender marriage, it's interesting how Massachusetts and California have figured into both discussions.

Over forty years later, I may still feel a twinge of reservation when I simply "see" a mixed race couple I have not come to know. Yet, interestingly, I never had that feeling when my friends Gina and Chris lived next door to me. She is Italian-American and he is African-American. This configuration of marriage was different from "the way it should be," according to ingrained prejudice, my gut reaction, but I never had an inkling as their neighbor that it was not "normal." Similarly, "Fred and Bob" or "Shirley and June" as neighbors or fellow church members help us see "their kind" differently, but not as wrong.

I believe that when human beings cannot identify the source of our discomfort about homosexuality, from whom or from where we learned our homophobia or heterosexism, we come to believe our feelings are natural, inborn, God-given. Opponents would be quick to say the same of homosexual feelings: since most lesbians and gay men report discovery rather than choice of our feelings, we come to believe our feelings are natural, inborn, God-given. The difference lies not only in the research of recent decades, which reveals sexual orientation of any kind is best understood as an unfolding, an unveiling in very early childhood related to a mix of factors, both genetic and psychosocial.[5] The difference also lies in the fact that, according to the school of thought of cultural anthropologist René Girard, we learn how to be human by imitation, by mimesis, mimicking others. The fact that homosexuals come from heterosexual parents, peers, churches, and cultures belies the notion of homosexuality as learned behavior. On the other hand, that children often hold the same prejudice as their parents, peers, church, or culture suggest we have learned such prejudice through the subtle process of imitation. As the Rodgers and Hammerstein song from *South Pacific* about racial prejudice suggests, we have to be carefully taught.

Just Plain Dirty

In his book, *Dirt, Greed, and Sex: Sexual Ethics in the New Testament and Their Implications for Today,* Episcopal priest and seminary professor L. William Countryman describes the sense of "dirty" applied to human behaviors in the Holiness Code of Leviticus, where two prohibitions on males acting like females in sexual intercourse occur, Leviticus 18:22 and 20:13. Personal integrity and social harmony are the general principles underlying both the moral laws (right and wrong) and ritual laws (pure and impure) of the Holiness Code. The laws presupposed orders of creation, categories of existence, that were not to be mixed up. A familiar example of not mixing things up are the kosher laws still practiced as a spiritual discipline by many Jews today: certain foods are not to be served nor stored with other foods. Other examples are the laws against sowing a field with two different kinds of seed, or wearing a garment made of two different materials; both are common practices today.

Countryman illustrates "dirty" with a rather tame example of a contemporary taboo: putting quarters in your mouth, a taboo most of us were taught not to do as children for fear of germs. But I want to use a more vivid example: picking your nose in public. As did many bodily functions, this taboo became the subject of a hilarious *Seinfeld* episode. A woman Seinfeld was interested in misinterprets him scratching his nose for picking his nose, and is so disgusted, she loses interest. Now, I hope I'm not revealing "too much information" to say that most of us have probably stuck a finger up our noses. But to be "caught with a finger up our nose" is an idiom suggesting profound embarrassment. Public nose-picking is taboo. It is not morally or legally wrong; it is just plain "dirty." As such, it elicits a visceral response. It's not like we haven't "been there, done that." But to witness it in public elicits feelings ranging, for most of us, from discomfort to repugnance. That is the nature of taboo. "What is consistent from one culture to another is that purity rules relate to the boundaries of the human body, especially to its orifices," Countryman writes.[6]

Countryman goes on to explain that this is the nature of the purity laws of ancient Israel. As with any culture, certain things or behaviors were considered "dirty." Men acting like women in the sex act was one of them. Having sex during menstruation was another. A seminal discharge yet another, and so on. As Catholic scholar Daniel Helminiak points out in *What the Bible Really Says About Homosexuality*, echoing John Boswell and others, the word used in Leviticus to describe such acts, translated as "abomination," is *toevah*, which could be accurately translated as "uncleanness," "impurity," "dirtiness," or "taboo"—in other words, what is forbidden culturally and ritually. Helminiak points out that another Hebrew word, *zimah*, could have been used to mean "what is wrong in itself. It means an injustice, a sin."[7] To underscore this careful delineation between what is understood as a sin versus a ritual violation, Helminiak adds that the Greek translation of Jewish scriptures, the Septuagint, translated the Hebrew *toevah* with the Greek *bdelygma*, which means ritual impurity, though other Greek words, such as *anomia*, which meant a violation of law or sin, could have been used.

With all the studies of lesbians and gay men these days, plus our own self-reporting about our experience, I have wondered why more people are not convinced that homosexuality is a natural variation of human sexuality. But I can better understand by looking carefully at one of my own taboos that comes from my childrearing: a toilet is "dirty," no matter how clean it looks or even is. By contrast, I view a kitchen counter as "clean," no matter what foodstuffs have been prepared on it, and even when it is slightly messy. Despite the fact that studies have revealed that the cleanest surface in a house is usually the toilet, I hold onto my notion that it is "dirty." In parallel fashion, we may view homosexuality as "dirty" no matter how loving, and heterosexuality as "clean" even when it is not as loving or as just in its expressions as we would expect. The vital difference in the analogous experiences of taboo, of course, is that mine doesn't interfere with how I view or relate to human beings.

Taboo and Shame

Contemporary writers in psychology and ethics make a distinction between guilt and shame. Guilt helps us take responsibility for our actions. Shame, in contrast, humiliates us to the point of believing ourselves incapable of taking responsibility for our actions, incapable of either confessing or correcting our sins. Whereas guilt suggests we are people who have done something bad, shame makes us feel like bad people. Though one might be ashamed of one's sin, taboos are *all about* shaming. A gay church member told me that the worst thing that a member of his conservative college campus group could say to another member was, "I will pray for you!" It meant something was seriously awry with the prayer victim's belief or behavior, and the words had the chilling effect of shaming the person for being different, an attempt to shame him or her into conformity. This shaming takes the form of formal and informal shunning in some expressions of Christianity, as in the apostle Paul's admonition to have nothing to do with such persons. When I began a gay Christian group on the Yale Divinity School campus in 1974, a Lutheran professor asked me, "What right do we have to tell these people they *shouldn't* be ashamed?" My response was, "Why do we feel we have the right to tell 'these people' they *should* be ashamed?—and we've been doing that for years!"

Shaming is what the men of Sodom were about in Genesis 19. The humiliation of rape was a common way to inflict shame on a defeated people in ancient times—raping not just the women, but the men as well. The intended gang rape of the angels by "*all* of the men" of the city of Sodom sealed its fate, to be destroyed by God for general wickedness. It is no more homosexual in orientation than similar rape in prisons. To treat a man as a woman in ancient times, or for a man to behave like a woman, was either to remove or relinquish superior male status. Apart from spilling seed outside a womb, another possible reason, this may be a basis for the Levitical taboo of (only) male homosexuality. Not long ago, this form of shaming was used by a few New York policemen accused of sodomizing a suspect with a broom handle, and by a few American soldiers in Iraq accused of sodomizing male captors with implements and photographing them naked in simulated homosexual group acts.

If one believes all the men of Sodom were homosexual, then logic would dictate the men in the above described incidents were also, a conclusion those men would undoubtedly protest. (I can't help but think that open gays in the military might help sensitize the armed services and make this type of behavior less likely. I also want to be clear that New York policemen and the American military as a whole should not be tarred with the same brush as the few perpetrators of these crimes, just as the few pedophile priests and ministers that have come to light should not prejudice us toward priests and ministers as a whole.)

An example of the importance of maintaining one's male status occurs when Jonathan chose, out of love for David, not to fight him and, instead, support him for his father's throne. King Saul viewed it as his son's degradation: "You have chosen the son of Jesse [David] to your own shame, and to the shame of your mother's nakedness" (1 Samuel 20:30). In other words, Jonathan has not behaved like a man, having surrendered his own power to another man. (This story will be discussed in more detail in Chapter Six.) Breaking out of gender conformity is another deeply held taboo, thus the sometimes viscerally negative response today exhibited toward transgender people, "effeminate" men, and "masculine" women.

Shame on Rome!

Toward the end of the first chapter of his letter to the church at Rome, the apostle Paul seems to be utilizing a rhetorical form of humiliation on Gentiles and their idolatry, in which he shames them by declaring they have debased *themselves* by controverting their "natural" gender and sexual roles:

> For what can be known about God is plain . . . but they became futile in their thinking. . . . Claiming to be wise, they became fools; and they exchanged the glory of the immortal God for images resembling a mortal human being or four footed animals or reptiles. Therefore God gave them up in the lusts of their hearts to impurity, to the degrading of their bodies among themselves, because they exchanged the truth about God for a lie

and worshiped and served the creature rather than the Creator,
who is blessed forever! Amen.

For this reason God gave them up to degrading passions.
Their women exchanged natural intercourse for unnatural, and
in the same way also the men, giving up natural intercourse with
women, were consumed with passion for one another. Men committed shameless acts with men and received in their own persons the due penalty for their error. And since they did not see fit
to acknowledge God, God gave them up to a debased mind and
to things that should not be done. They were filled with every
kind of wickedness . . ." (Romans 1:19a; 21c, 22–29a)

Then Paul finishes up by listing every kind of wickedness he can think
of, though not a list unique to Paul and similar to the moralizers of his
time who would say "that's not the way it should be." It is also similar
to the standard laundry list of sins in 1 Corinthians 6:9–11, which
includes a couple of words whose meaning has been debated over the
centuries, and will be discussed in the next chapter.

I quote so much of this first chapter of Romans because the more
one reads of it, the more one may recognize that Paul's tone in this sec-
tion is at odds with the point of this and others of his letters. The apostle prefaces this viciously shaming diatribe with the theme of the letter,
which is salvation by grace through faith: "For I am not ashamed of the
gospel," Paul declares in Romans 1:16, and then quotes Habakkuk 2:4:
"The one who is righteous will live by faith." Apparently Paul is writing
because some in the Roman church have resented the fact that others
are not following Jewish law, the legalists essentially saying, "that's not
the way it should be." Notice his emphasis on impurity, the violation
of ritual law.

Quite apart from what additional biblical scholarship might bring
to the passage, and apart from the psychological aspect of choosing
against one's own nature, whether heterosexual or homosexual—if one
were to observe simply the literary form of this "over-the-top" condemnation, one could conclude that Paul was up to something quite
other than what initially meets the eye or ear. The reader familiar with
other Pauline writings could conclude that the evangelist who said he

would become all things to all people so that they might prove receptive to the gospel is not about to alienate the Gentiles, to whom he felt especially sent. To make plain his purpose, Paul turns the tables on his legalist opponent ("that's not the way it should be") at the beginning of chapter 2: "Therefore you have no excuse, whoever you are, when you judge others; for in passing judgment on another you condemn yourself, because you, the judge, are doing the very same things." The effect is to shame those who oppose the new freedom in Christ.

A straight Christian ally once told me that she thought that the reason the church had not dealt fairly with lesbians and gay men was because Christians had not been adequately shamed for their mistreatment. I appreciated her sentiment, while disagreeing with her method. Shaming is a way of silencing the other, and silence, to paraphrase the adage, does not necessarily mean agreement. As a member of a minority that has been shamed and silenced too long, I don't want to employ the same weapons on those who oppose us. Audré Lorde admonished us not to dismantle the master's house with the master's tools. And the fact is, opponents voice the questions the answers to which more moderate Christians want to know but may be afraid to ask. In truth, they ask the very questions for which most lesbian and gay Christians are either actively seeking or have already sought answers. That's why gay and lesbian and bisexual and transgender Christians can be helpful in the dialogue on sexuality and gender and marriage, ranging from biblical authority and interpretation to sexual and marital ethics.

Part of the intensity of the discussion of homosexuality comes from our feelings that homosexuality is dirty and something of which we are to be ashamed, whether we are homosexual ourselves or a member of a homosexual person's biological or church family. Thus parents, siblings, and children of gay people fall under the same shadow of shame. "What did we do wrong?" parents, spouses, even children may ask. And "What will the neighbors think?" is not only a question family members might ask. "What will other denominations think?" has been a question posed by governing bodies asked to change church policies. Because neither the church nor the therapeutic profession can honestly or ethically promise change of sexual orientation, there is no "rite of reconciliation" to lift the church and culture out of this shame *unless our attitudes about homosexuality themselves change*—in other words, unless our customs are reformed, and this taboo alleviated by putting in place rights and protection for same gender marriages.

Unsavory Associations

Taboos reinforce one another. As a former Baptist, I relish the old joke about why Baptists object to intercourse while standing: it might lead to dancing! The discredited domino theory once applied to communism is now applied to homosexuality. "If this taboo falls, it will start a chain reaction." During the years I served on a denominational task force on homosexuality, I heard many references to "opening Pandora's Box." Pandora is the "Eve" of Greek mythology, in that she too was the first woman on earth, and her curiosity that opened the box released all evils on earth, much as Eve led the way (to some people's way of thinking) to the introduction of original sin. Both stories clearly come from a patriarchal point of view. Few remember that one good remained behind in Pandora's box: Hope. Similarly, the lineage of Eve would give rise to liberators and prophets, to the Redeemer and the saints—in other words, to hope.

In *Christianity, Social Tolerance, and Homosexuality*, medieval historian John Boswell documents that, though homosexuality was tolerated and even acceptable at various points of church history, when it was challenged, it was often given unsavory associations, such as bestiality and child abduction. This is done today in a "rational" attempt to explain our pre-rational taboos, our gut feelings about "the way things should be." Taboos are strongest when linked together. So today many in the Roman Catholic hierarchy, rather than take responsibility for their own cover-ups of pedophile priests who abused either boys or girls, condemn gay priests, as if pedophilia is more common among gay people than among straight people, something studies have not borne out.

Perhaps the most all-encompassing unsavory association in what social psychologists generally consider a sex-negative culture such as ours in the United States is homosexuality's association with sexuality itself, an area with which the church and culture have difficulties. I was part of a regional church legislative body voting on a proposal to open ordination "regardless of sexual orientation." The vote was tied, 69 to 69. The moderator of the meeting chose to cast the deciding ballot. After a show of clear embarrassment, he voted against the measure, "because," he said, "of those three little letters at its heart: s-e-x." He couldn't even *say* the word! In that moment, centuries of Christian and cultural attitudes toward sexuality came crashing down on gay people. Consider a few examples: the unmarried Paul's grudging acceptance, "it is better to marry than to be aflame with passion" (1 Corinthians 7:9); the elevation of celibacy as the most desirable lifestyle and of the perpetually virgin (in the Catholic view) Mary as role model, especially for women; the focus of marital intercourse on procreation, the *only* justification for sexuality in more than one church patriarch's view; and John Calvin's warning against being aflame with passion even within marriage (Institutes of the Christian Religion, Book II, Chapter VII, 44, "Modesty and Chastity."). More of this background will be presented in subsequent chapters.

Further evidence of shame surrounding sexuality is the devastation felt by those who contract sexually transmitted diseases, often making them feel all the more "dirty," though all of these are curable or treatable. The association of AIDS with gay men, and the association of AIDS with premature death, promotes the notion that homosexuality is "dirty," with additional unsavory associations with three other cultural taboos: disease, suffering, and death. An opponent's chief ploy debating me on the subject of homosexuality in front of a church governing body in Colorado was that gay men were "disease-ridden," illustrating his case with a hypothetical house of gay men and how many would have this disease or that disease, based on his own "statistics."

Regulating Sexuality

Sexuality is truly a power to be reckoned with. It is associated with *eros*, what I term "the urge to merge," the desire to be one with the beloved. It is commonly contrasted with *agape*, the benevolent love celebrated in Christian scripture, which may be bestowed even upon enemies. Though Boswell and others have indicated that the words were often used interchangeably in Greek texts,[8] the contrast has nonetheless proven useful in discussing nuances of love. Yet what would surprise many people is that both sexuality and spirituality are fueled by *eros*, the desire to be one with the beloved. For the lover, this is accomplished in lovemaking and marriage. For the mystic, this is accomplished in prayermaking and communion with God. *Agape*, "the will to extend one's self for the purpose of nurturing one's own or another's spiritual growth,"[9] is the benevolent, Christian love that governs *eros*, whether the *eros* of sexuality or spirituality.

Sexually, *eros* ungoverned by *agape* may lead to imposed physical "intimacy": rape. Spiritually, *eros* ungoverned by *agape* may lead to an imposed spiritual "unity": coerced conformity. Even the apostle Paul, while wishing others to be like him, allowed alternate choices in sexual and other matters. "For freedom Christ has set us free . . . do not submit again to a yoke of slavery," tradition holds that Paul wrote in Galatians 5:1.

Though justified by Christ, Christians are nonetheless to grow in faith, a process known as sanctification. There may be a tension between justification (righteousness through Christ by faith) and sanctification (the Christian striving toward perfection), with one sometimes getting emphasized to the detriment of the other. Conservative Reformed scholar John Leith admits the following liabilities, which, though applied here to the Reformed tradition, may be applied to the broader Christian tradition:

> In practical life, however, Calvin and the Reformed tradition often failed to maintain the tension and overemphasized sanctification. One result has been legalism, which in the end always lacks grace. Another result has been self-righteousness, especially when sin is reduced to sensuality, which is more manageable than pride or apathy, especially in old age. A third consequence has been obscurantism [opposition to human progress or enlightenment] when the will of God is prematurely identified with some human pattern of conduct.[10] [Definition added.]

I cannot help but draw parallels with the legalism and self-righteousness that so readily rejects LGBT Christians, and an obscurantism that identifies one particular marriage expression with God's will.

Sex Negativity

Some readers might wonder at the earlier reference of American culture as sex-negative when we are bombarded with sexual stimuli on a daily basis, from billboards to Super Bowl halftime shows. But the lurid and titillating and often manipulative way in which sex is introduced implies the shadowy place it has in our imagination. C. S. Lewis once pointed out that a stripper on stage might be compared to a gourmet meal hidden from view by a lid that is slowly, tantalizingly lifted for a few seconds, and then covered again, lifted once more, and so on, to the rhythms of seductive music. If we had a wholesome view of sex and the body, the stripper concept would seem as dull and absurd. Catholic theologian Mary Hunt has said she looks forward to the day when we all feel as comfortable placing a package of condoms in our grocery carts as we do milk and eggs.

I was first introduced to this concept of our culture's sex negativity by a regular presenter to the educational conferences that we organized under the auspices of the Lazarus Project, a ministry of reconciliation between the church and the LGBT community funded by the Presbyterian Church and located at West Hollywood Presbyterian Church in California. Dr. Richard Smith, a professor in social psychology at my alma mater, California State University at Northridge, illustrated our culture's sex negativity with our choice of profanity: often, words about sex. These words have strength as profanity because they are taboo, as indeed, are many of the activities they represent. If we regarded the words and activities in a neutral or a positive way, they would lose their power as profanity. Without scandalizing readers by being explicit, I encourage the reader to consider how even the least questionable sexual practices are nonetheless used as negative appellations. In a sex-positive society, such comments would be terms of endearment! Smith used to say we might even cheerfully greet one another with phrases we presently use to antagonize one another.

I began utilizing this analysis as the basis of a workshop exercise in which I invited people to speak out words of profanity (a real icebreaker, by the way). As people sheepishly offer them, I list them, without explanation, in three columns. At the end of the naming of profane words,

I title the columns: Sex and Body, Spirit and Religion, Stranger and The Other. In other words, what I have come to realize is that most of our profanity comes out of the realms of sexuality and the body, spirituality and religion, and xenophobia (fear of the stranger or the other). We are not only a sex-negative society, we are a body-negative and spirit-negative and stranger-negative society. All of them reflect some form of taboo as well, and are used to shame the victim of our profanity. We refer to people negatively as body parts, especially strong if we refer to lower extremity orifices. We take the Lord's name in vain, we "damn" people or tell them "to go to hell." We have pejorative terms for racial, ethnic, sexual, and gender minorities, women as well as men, people with disabilities and people of other nationalities. Please also note that the profane words for which I feel most comfortable citing specific examples are those having to do with God and spirituality!

Sometimes those in the third category of stranger are also associated with the first two categories. One of the things the writer of *Black Like Me* discovered, for example, was that upon darkening his skin color, white men were more likely to talk with him about sex in explicit and vulgar terms, either because they thought black men were "more" sexual or because they didn't care what black men thought of them, or both. (Frankly, I've had similar experiences as a gay man with straight men and women, though part of this comes from the positive phenomenon that "coming out" begets "coming out," as I've written in another context.[11]) Another example of this commingling of categories is that pejorative terms for women and men often make reference to their genitals or their sexual expression or their gender ambiguity.

My biggest "aha," however, was that people who are gay, lesbian, bisexual, and transgender figured into all three categories. Not only are we "the other" or "the stranger," we are associated more strongly with sexuality and the body, especially sexual behavior and bodily parts that are particularly taboo. And those of us who affirm our spirituality are especially set upon, by our communities of faith, obviously, but also by our own LGBT community, that, until recently, has frequently ignored or rejected us as well. A simple illustration of this phenomenon is that the original subtitle of my first book, "A Gay Christian's Struggle to Serve the Church" was changed in 1988 by its first publisher to "A Gay

Man's Struggle to Serve the Church," because, I was told, "gay Christian" sounded too much like an oxymoron. Only its second publisher allowed a return to the original subtitle in the expanded edition of 1996.

There may be some comfort for the heterosexual majority placing LGBT people in the third category of "other" or "stranger." It can segregate us from the mainstream, from normality, from the dominant culture's neighborhoods and churches, from its institutions of ministry, military, marriage, and family. Though it may sometimes be disconcerting dealing with "the other," perhaps even *more* disconcerting for the general public are those of us who claim we are not so very different from those of the mainstream. When we want to be neighbors and fellow church members, to serve in the ministry and the military, as teachers and scoutmasters, and finally, to be married and rear children—this, in many ways, is more challenging to "the way things should be." As Christian ethicist Marvin Ellison refutes the critique of marriage among some gay activists:

> It is not when gay people press, but rather when they *give up*, their claim on marriage (and other institutions) that they most conform to the dominant culture's rules and expectations. Accordingly, seeking the legal (and religious) right to marry may not be at all assimilationist, but rather a confrontational challenge to the heterosexist marriage monopoly that refuses to acknowledge the human dignity and rights of nonheterosexual people.[12]

Shifting Paradigms

James B. Nelson, who, as a Christian "body theologian"[13]—one who tries to recover an embodied spirituality—has written much on the relationship of sexuality and spirituality. He suggests it is the very association of gay men with sexuality that makes many straight men uncomfortable. There is, of course, the fear of being "objectified" as sexual objects, much as straight men may objectify women. And there is also the fear of "womanization," the assumption that in a male-male relationship, one assumes the subordinate role of the woman, a heresy to a patriarchal mindset. But Nelson, himself a heterosexual male, claims an additional and deeper fear:

A related dynamic is my envy of gays' sexual power. . . . I am one whose conditioning makes him think that the real man is always ready for sex, that he can never get enough of it, and that his potency is the ultimate symbol of his manliness. . . . While in my conscious stereotype, I think of the gay male as "less of a man" than I, in the confusions of my homophobic unconscious, I see him as *more* male than I. Homosexuality, particularly gay homo-sexuality, has become the primary symbol of sexual energy and potency, freely expressed. It has become the primary symbol of potency, of the one who is always ready. Thus, in a strange way, the gay male is more male than I, and that is the occasion for rage.[14]

Nelson challenges "the way things should be" in *The Intimate Connection* by offering a helpful schema for the way many people in the West, particularly Christians, view the world. It is a view inherited in part from Judaism, definitively influenced by Hellenism (Greek thought, especially Stoicism), but for which we must take full responsibility as Christians. Its main perspective is a dualism that separates spirit and body, spirituality and sexuality, reason and feelings, mind and matter. Nelson claims that any dualism implies a hierarchy, that one is considered better than the other, that the higher must control the lower. We can see it in the pure/impure dualism that informs the Holiness Code of Leviticus. Thus we think that spirit must control body, spirituality must reign over sexuality, reason must override feelings, and that mind must triumph over matter. "Pure" spirit, spirituality, reason, and mind are "masculine" attributes associated with a Father God. "Impure" body, sexuality, feelings, and matter are "female" attributes associated with Mother Earth.

So God is on top of what Nelson depicts as "a pyramid of control" with a descending hierarchy beneath "him." Males are right there just below God, because God has male attributes. What follows in the descending order of hierarchy (a word which literally means "holy order") are women, children, other races (an addition I have made to Nelson's analysis, because other races are often viewed as inferior to the dominant race), animals (viewed as "soulless"), vegetation, organic material, inorganic material. God is on top and earth is the bottom of the hierarchy. In a hierarchy, higher levels exercise power and control over lower levels.[15]

One need not be either a rocket scientist or a brain surgeon to recognize that this "plan" chances wreaking havoc in terms of social relations between men and women, adults and children, and among races, let alone what it may do to the ecology of the planet. Yet, when I presented this paradigm during a regional retreat for Disciples of Christ ministers, one minister told me that, honestly, if he presented this to his congregation, most would say, "What's wrong with that?" God is in "his" heaven, and everything is right with the world.

It is this pattern of understanding that leads many well-meaning Christians to say to LGBT Christians, "Deny your sexuality (or your gender) for the sake of your spirituality. Deny your bodily desires (or your gender identity) so that your spirit may rise. Relinquish the 'impure' for the 'pure,' the earthly for the heavenly." Like women in this paradigm, LGBT people, in affirming our bodies, our sexuality (or gender identity), and our feelings are associated with the lowest echelon of the hierarchy, Earth. The dominant culture controls us, and we must control our desires, thus denying our true identities and our loving relationships.

We have only to open our newspapers to realize that this worldview is not working. We have only to open our Bibles, particularly the Gospels, to realize this worldview is not in sync with Jesus or God's will for humanity. God, who became flesh, descending from the awesome heavens to the depths of Sheol out of love for us, is One who apparently has little regard for hierarchy. Jesus said to call no one "rabbi" or "father" on earth. "The greatest shall be the least of all," he admonished in a variety of contexts, and in the Gospel of John, he washes the disciples' feet to prove the point. Later, in the Acts of the Apostles, the early Christians are described by opponents as "those who are turning the world upside down." The world is still being turned upside down by the Christian message when it is not somehow co-opted or compromised. Down through the ages, I believe the "revolution" has continued in multiple forms that question "the way things should be."

There is some truth to the intuitive, gut feeling of opponents that the advent of same-gender marriage signals, not the destruction, but at least a "makeover" of the social fabric of society. Embracing Gentiles and democracy, addressing racism and sexism in earlier contexts signaled the reweaving of that same cloth. But Christians should not be surprised or offended or feel terror at such change. According to Paul, in a passage largely concerned about changing notions of marriage, "the present form of this world is passing away (1 Corinthians 7:31)," because Jesus himself initiated a different view of reality. Just as, at his death by crucifixion, the temple curtain veiling the Holy of Holies was torn in two from top to bottom, so his life and his teaching tore at the fabric of religion and culture.

Jesus and Taboo

Ultimately, Christians have to look behind scripture and culture and our own attitudes for the Word of God, Jesus Christ. Jesus turned the tables not only on the money changers of the temple at Jerusalem, but on the religious authorities of his time and of our own time. The kingdom of heaven was not to be found among the rich and privileged, but among the poor and religious outcasts. The next chapter will include fresh ways in which Jesus and those who followed him viewed marriage, procreation, and family, but of present interest to us is the way Jesus addressed the issue of taboo and ritual impurity and people's visceral responses to them. In a sense, Jesus wallowed in ritual impurity. Not that he sinned by our present standards, but he did "sin" by the standards of those who enforced "the way things should be"—all because he dined with, visited, touched, and allowed himself to be touched by the ritually impure. Such fraternizing would have rendered him ritually unclean. By doing so, he became what Amanda Udis-Kessler terms "the holy leper."[16]

Much of his taboo behavior has to do with the human boundaries and orifices of which William Countryman has been quoted: "What is consistent from one culture to another is that purity rules relate to the boundaries of the human body, especially to its orifices." Eating involves the mouth, and the spiritually "superior" would be cautious about impurity even dining with their own kind, let alone with those they called "sinners," with whom Jesus dined. Jesus touched the ears of the deaf and made mud from spit from his mouth to place on a blind man's eyes. He touched the leprous skin of a number of lepers, skin being the boundary of the body. He allowed himself to be touched by a hemorrhaging woman (perhaps menstruation gone awry), a contact condemned as unclean in Leviticus. He did not fear going to a cemetery to raise Lazarus, though contact with a corpse would defile a holy man. And he received the ministrations of a woman of ill repute who sensually washed his feet with her tears, dried them with her hair, and then "continued kissing his feet and anointing them with the ointment," to the consternation and condemnation of the Pharisee with whom Jesus dined (Luke 7:36–50).

The Pharisees often shamed him for eating with "tax collectors and sinners" as in Matthew 9:10–13, to which he replied with a quote from Hosea, "Go and learn what this means: 'I desire mercy, and not sacrifice'" (Hosea 6:6). An additional reason that he gave in this circumstance, "Those who are well have no need of a physician," has been understood to mean that he is among them to heal such sinners. But remember, in Christianity, "all have sinned and fall short of the glory of God" (Romans 3:23), part of Paul's continuing argument with the smugly self-righteous legalist mentioned earlier. And Jesus saved virtually all of his judgmental rhetoric for the self-righteous, who imagined themselves "pure." Most of the twenty-third chapter of Matthew is devoted to Jesus' vitriol against the super-religious "scribes and Pharisees" who appear pure on the outside but are impure on the inside. So the sinners with whom Jesus dined were no more sinful than the Pharisees. I believe he was there as a physician to heal the wounds of spiritual abuse, restoring the unfairly condemned "impure" religious outcasts to Yahweh, the God of their people.

In Mark 7:1–23, the religious leaders faulted his disciples for not washing their hands before eating—literally they did not "baptize their hands." Jesus responds that it is not what goes into a person that is spiritually vital, but what comes out of a person's heart. This seems a direct attack on purity laws, on what is taboo. They have to do with the outside; God has to do with the inside. They have to do with outward conformity; God looks on the heart for intentions. They have to do with human boundaries; God has to do with the love and will of the heart. The apostle Paul declares that even if he gave away all his possessions, or handed over his body to be burned, presumably in sacrifice, "but do not have love, I gain nothing" (1 Corinthians 13:3). Outward show does not mean inner purity. Outward form is not as spiritually vital as content, so "be not conformed to this world" (Romans 12:2).

The premise of some who argue against same-gender marriage is that form determines content when, in the Christian view, the content must be judged independent of form, just as the Reverend Marin Luther King Jr. had a dream of a day when his children would be judged by the content of their character rather than the color of their skin. Marriages would best be judged by the content of their character rather than the gender of their partners. Paul's frequent admonitions regarding the life "of the flesh," is often read in sensual terms. But what he means by "of the flesh" is anything that stands over against God. It is more likely a sense of purity and spiritual superiority that will serve as our fatally arrogant Tower of Babel, thinking we may build and climb on our own into God's heaven, believing we may earn our salvation.

"Teacher, what must I do to inherit eternal life?" a scholar of religious law asked Jesus in Luke 16. Jesus asked him what the law required. The lawyer responded with the traditional summary about loving God with all one's heart and mind and soul and strength, and to love one's neighbor as one's self. Jesus tells him, "Do this, and you will live." The scripture tells us that the questioner, "wanting to justify himself," asked, "And who is my neighbor?" Most readers will remember the parable of the Good Samaritan that follows. What is significant in terms of understanding Jesus' critique of purity laws is that the priest and Levite (lay priest, or elder) pass by the victim of robbers on the other side of the road to Jerusalem probably because they are going to the temple, and might be defiled if the person is sick or dead. The Samaritan has no such compunction, and shows him mercy. Now the Samaritans were considered unclean by Jesus' Jewish hearers, a mixed race whose worship differed from theirs. The idea of a "good Samaritan" would have been considered an oxymoron as "gay Christian" is to some today. Once again, Jesus confronts his listeners' visceral response to taboo, challenging the way things should be.

A gut objection to homosexuality and same-gender marriage may have its origins in an ancient and otherwise ignored purity system (at least by the church and most of society) that divides the pure from the impure, based on condition, race, gender, and category, as well as behavior that *mixes* conditions, race, gender, and categories. Christians must critically evaluate all and particular taboos in the light of the practice, teachings, and atoning (at-one-ing) effects of Jesus Christ, in whom, according to Paul's letter to the Galatians, "There is no longer Jew or Greek, there is no longer slave or free, there is no longer male and female . . ." (Galatians 3:28). In other words, we need to go deep within scripture to find God's Word to us. In the storm of controversy swirling around homosexuality and same-gender marriage, Christians may listen for Jesus' still, small voice, "Peace! Be still! Why are you afraid? Have you still no faith?" (Mark 4:39–40).

Notes

[1] Witte, Jr., *From Sacrament to Contract*, 217.

[2] Contemporary researchers are more aware than their predecessors of the bias of earlier studies, and thus are more likely to devise studies that minimalize bias.

[3] William Sloane Coffin, "Let Us Be Impatient With Prejudice," *Open Hands,* Vol. 16, No. 1 (Summer 2002), 25. Previously published January 20, 2000, in the *Rutland* (VT) *Herald,* during Vermont's debate on same-gender marriage vs. civil unions. Coffin, a Presbyterian and former pastor of New York's Riverside Church, argued for full marriage rights.

[4] Ellison, *Same-Sex Marriage?*, 14.

[5] See Chandler Burr, "Homosexuality and Biology," *The Atlantic Monthly* (Vol. 271, No. 3, March 1993). Burr later developed this article into a book entitled *A Separate Creation: The Search for the Biological Origins of Sexual Orientation* (New York: Hyperion, 1996).

[6] L. William Countryman, *Dirt, Greed, and Sex: Sexual Ethics in the New Testament and Their Implications for Today* (Minneapolis, MN: Augsburg Fortress, 1988). See especially Chapter One, "What Is Purity?" Quote is from page 13.

[7] Daniel A. Helminiak, Ph.D., *What the Bible Really Says About Homosexuality* (San Francisco: Alamo Square Press, 1994), 52.

[8] John Boswell, *Same-Sex Unions in Premodern Europe* (New York: Villard Books, 1994), Chapter 1.

[9] M. Scott Peck, *The Road Less Traveled* (New York: Simon & Schuster, 1978), 81. I am using Peck's definition of love as the best interpretation of *agape*.

[10] John H. Leith, *Introduction to the Reformed Tradition* (Atlanta: John Knox Press, 1977), 77.

[11] Chris Glaser, *Coming Out as Sacrament* (Louisville, KY: Westminster John Knox Press, 1998).

[12] Ellison, *Same-Sex Marriage?*, 123.

[13] Body theologians make up a present-day Christian movement that seeks to correct the notion of spirituality as an "out of body" experience, affirming the body and sexuality as holy gifts from God. An excellent compendium of sample writings of a wide range of body theologians is the tome *Sexuality and the Sacred: Sources for Theological Reflection* (Louisville, KY: Westminster/John Knox Press, 1994).

[14] James B. Nelson, *The Intimate Connection: Male Sexuality, Masculine Spirituality* (Philadelphia: The Westminster Press, 1988), 61–62.

[15] I can't resist offering Boswell's humorous counter to such a hierarchy in one of his presentations for the Lazarus Project. He pointed out that in the first chapter of Genesis, God created plants, animals, man, and woman in a clearly *ascending* order of importance!

[16] Amanda Udis-Kessler, "The Holy Leper and the Bisexual Christian," *Open Hands*, Vol. 14, No. 1 (Summer 1998), 8. She references two books by Marcus Borg, *Meeting Jesus Again for the First Time: The Historical Jesus and the Heart of Contemporary Faith* (New York: Harper Collins, 1994), Chapter 3; and *Jesus, A New Vision: Spirit, Culture and the Life of Discipleship* (New York: HarperCollins, 1987), Chapter 5.

CHAPTER THREE

Traditional Family Values

Marriage, Procreation, and Family

"Who is my mother, and who are my brothers?" And pointing to his disciples, [Jesus] said, "Here are my mother and my brothers! For whoever does the will of my Father in heaven is my brother and sister and mother."
— Matthew 12:48b–50

For more than half of church history, marriage, procreation, and the biological family were relatively unimportant to Christians. The proclamation of the gospel, the inbreaking kingdom of heaven, and the anticipated imminent return of Jesus Christ predicated a sexuality that was not concerned with preserving biological family ties, entering into marriage, and the birthing and rearing of children. The tenor was like that of the ancient Hebrews preparing to leave Egypt immediately, not even taking time to leaven their bread. There wasn't time to marry or to have children. Celibacy and virginity were the higher if not highest spiritual values when it came to sexuality, practiced individually, in a monastic community, and even within marriage itself.

If they did marry, the early Christians adopted the ostensibly monogamous marriage pattern of Rome, an economic or civil arrangement rather than an ecclesiastical affair, usually for the privileged classes. And, though some of these may have been blessed informally by the marriage partners' parish priest, the first heterosexual marriage ceremonies were not performed officially within church walls until the thirteenth century. According to historian John Boswell, a Roman Catholic, "Heterosexual marriage was regarded as a compromise with the material world . . . in the West the church made very little effort to regulate marriage before the tenth century, and only declared it a sacrament and required ecclesiastical involvement in 1215."[1] Later, the rise of Protestantism in the sixteenth century influenced the consigning of marriage to the governments of the emerging nation-states of Europe. Protestants rejected marriage as a sacrament before God, and wanted the state to provide the necessary ordering of the institution.[2]

Ancient Roots

The story goes that two married women were sitting in church, listening to their celibate priest's pious homily on marriage. Afterward, one said to the other, "I wish I knew as little about marriage as he does!"

In 1996, as I witnessed with aversion a twice-divorced and thrice-married U.S. Congressman introduce the Defense of Marriage Act to preclude same-gender marriage and a philandering President sign it into law, I realized how little even those who are married may know about it, even while gaining political capital by keeping it exclusive.

Stephanie Coontz reminds us of the Roman Emperor Augustus who contrived political advantages through a convoluted series of coerced divorces and remarriages. Augustus, she writes, then "became a fervent public supporter of family stability. . . . Like many contemporary boosters of the sanctity of marriage, he did not let his own divorce and many sexual liaisons inhibit him from trying to impose marital virtue and 'family values' on others. In fact, Augustus embarked upon one of the earliest promarriage campaigns in the historical record."[3]

Opponents of same-gender marriage are quick to point out that it was Adam and Eve, not Adam and Steve, who cohabited in Eden. But the Bereshit Rabah, an ancient Hebrew *midrash* (interpretive text) on the Genesis creation accounts, suggests that the first human creature was androgynous, and the reference to taking a rib is better understood as taking a side of the first to create the second human creature.[4]

There is a similar mythological understanding in Hellenistic culture. The ancient Greek philosopher Plato (fourth century B.C.E.), a student of Aristotle and the teacher of Socrates, wrote *The Symposium*, a dialogue of Aristotle and other philosophers about the nature of love. One of them, Aristophenes, invoked a myth explaining opposite-gender and same-gender couples. Individuals came from double-bodied people, each with four legs, four arms, two heads, and so on, in the following configurations: double men, double women, and a man and woman. The gods divided them, and since then they have sought counterparts to match the gender of their original partner, man with man, woman with woman, and man with woman.[5]

"Aristotle describes as admirable—but not bizarre and unexpected—a pair of male lovers who spent their whole lives together, maintaining a single household, and arranged to be buried beside each other,"[6] Boswell writes, adding, "Doubtless the most surprising and counterintuitive aspect of Greek same-sex eroticism was not its frequency or duration, but its long and hallowed relationship to democracy and military valor, which modern military officials tend to find improbable or even unbelievable."[7] In *Love Between Women*, Bernadette Brooten, professor of Christian studies at Brandeis University, documents references to woman–woman marriage in Egypt as early as the second or early third century C.E.[8]

Coontz writes that "the Greek model for true love was not the relationship of a husband and a wife" but between two men, and quotes historian Eve Cantarella that a male Athenian "expressed his better side, intelligence, will for self-improvement, and a higher level of emotions" in dignified homosexual relations.[9] In his own persuasive argument, Boswell concludes, "Most ancient writers—in striking opposition to their modern counterparts—generally entertained higher expectations of the fidelity and permanence of homosexual passions than of heterosexual feelings."[10]

Biblical Variations on Marriage

Marriage is an elastic term. I prefer the adjective "elastic" because it implies a bond that wraps around the partners in a marriage firmly, and yet stretches to fit various kinds of arrangements. I am not inventing something here, merely depicting our human ability to wrap our minds around very different forms of human relationship and still call them marriage. Those who think marriage has but one form have only to look into their Bibles. Adam and Eve were made for each other, could be said to enjoy God's blessing, but had no religious ceremony and no legal contract (Genesis 2). Abram's wife, Sarai, gave Hagar to her husband "as a wife" (Genesis 16:3), because she had not borne him an heir. Jacob was tricked into marrying Leah, but then married his true interest, Rachel, as well (Genesis 29:15–30). King David had "at least twenty concubines and wives, [and] was apparently never criticized on this score."[11] King Solomon reportedly had at least 700 wives and 300 concubines (1 Kings 11:3), and the only complaint surrounding this feat was that they turned his head to gods other than Yahweh, the God of Israel. Polygamy was a traditional marriage value in ancient Israel and the overwhelming majority of other cultures as well. Jewish law *assumed* the possibility of multiple wives, as evidenced by Deuteronomy 21:15, which explains what to do in terms of inheritance if the man prefers one wife to another.

The notion of marriage for reasons of romantic love gained ascendancy only in recent centuries, and is not practiced universally even today. Most Hindu marriages in India, for example, are still arranged by the families involved, with a much lower divorce rate than in the United States. Many other examples from different eras and cultures have been exhaustively compiled in a recent book by the earlier cited Stephanie Coontz, a professor of history and family studies: *Marriage, A History: How Love Conquered Marriage.*[12]

Prior to the equation of love and marriage, "lovers" were generally thought to be illicit or adulterous affairs. Even today the term "lovers" carries this connotation, so that, when partners in gay or lesbian relationships refer to their spouse as "lover," there is yet another unsavory association with an illicit sexual union, unintended though it may be. A straight ally attending a church conference I helped organize about LGBT people reflected on the day by saying he felt uncomfortable with our references to "lovers" until he realized he was sitting next to *his* lover, his wife!

Prior to romance, economics and politics were primary reasons for marriage, but within the privileged classes: "Until relatively late in European history [lower-class] unions were rarely recognized by the law or accorded much public significance."[13] Again, we need only look to scripture for examples of marriage for economic or political reasons. Ruth loved her mother-in-law, Naomi, and maneuvered Boaz into a marriage that would support them both financially, including the "social security" of progeny. King Saul's heir, Jonathan, loved David, and their friendship, along with David's perhaps politically calculated marriage to Saul's daughter Michal, helped legitimate David's ambitious quest for their father's throne. (We will revisit these stories in Chapter Six.)

Women were not citizens in ancient Israel, they were property. The husband obtained her by paying a "bride price" to her father, as in Genesis 34:12. Divorce was permitted, not on the wife's initiative, but by the husband's choice, who was simply required to give her notice of the divorce and permission to remarry in writing, presumably returning the bride price to her father's family.[14] As all sins, adultery in ancient Israel was a sin against God, but one given prominence by its inclusion in the Ten Commandments. It was not a sin against a marriage vow, such as fidelity, a virtue not necessarily expected of a male. Rather, it was a sin of stealing another man's possession, his wife. Thus it's listed between two other commandments about stealing: another man's life ("You shall not murder" [Exodus 20:13]) and another man's possessions (You shall not steal" [Exodus 20:15]). Adultery also prevented certain knowledge of the women's progeny as legitimate heirs of the husband's and the husband's family property. Though there could be love in marriage, marriage was primarily concerned with the preservation of the husband's property and inheritance. When a brother died without an heir, his brother was *obligated* by Jewish law to have intercourse with her, and the child so conceived would be considered the progeny of the dead brother, thus the heir, as well as the welfare provider for his mother's old age.

Though Onan's sin came to be used against masturbation, the scripture is clear that his true sin was disobedience to God's command to have intercourse with his brother's wife, instead, "spilling his seed" on the ground. The actual Hebrew means "destroying his seed." To the ancient Hebrews, destroying the seed was destroying life that, inside the mother's womb, would come to fruition, the Hebrews (alongside other ancient peoples) having an incomplete knowledge of the woman's role in the reproductive process. Paradoxically, if the seed didn't produce offspring, the woman rather than the man was blamed and shamed as "barren." Could ancient Hebrews have thought that her womb had destroyed the seed?

Biblically, procreation was not the sole purpose of marriage. But the laws (such as the one that compelled Onan) and the polygamous nature of marriage (which included multiple wives and concubines) were designed to ensure multiple baby delivery systems. Infant mortality was high; diseases, malnutrition, dehydration, violence, and war took their toll on children, youth, and adults; and the population of an initially nomadic and frequently warring and, at times, subjugated people had to be replaced. Anyone who didn't pull his or her weight in the baby-making business would have been viewed as "unpatriotic."

Rabbinic tradition holds that all Jewish laws can be traced to the original Ten Commandments. Thus the rule against male homosexual practice is said to have been derived from the commandment—no, not the one on adultery—but from "You shall not murder." The seed was life. To spill it outside a womb was to "destroy" progeny. Now that we know that the seed must fertilize an egg, the prohibition makes less sense. Even this knowledge does not prevent us from debating when life begins when it comes to the delicate issue of abortion.

Catholic scholar Bernadette Brooten has pointed out that the apostle Paul, a conservative Jewish zealot before conversion, uses the Greek word for "married" in Romans 7:2 which literally translates "under a man," a common usage among Greek and Latin writers of his time.[15] Although the word refers to the "proper" form of sexual intercourse, metaphorically it represents once again the man dominating and possessing the woman.

Though women's status would be advanced by the advent of the Jesus movement, with women playing significant roles in Jesus' ministry and in the early church, the notion of men's ownership of women survived through the centuries, finding its way into early civil laws regulating marriage,[16] and lingers still within contemporary attitudes. The father is said to "give away" the bride, walking his daughter down the aisle to the next man to take possession of her. The husband, itself a term indicating his proprietorship of her fertility, has "asked for her hand in marriage," and then takes possession.

Though marriage might have joined families in an economic or political relationship or both, the marriage partners themselves initially did not "become one flesh" as might be supposed: the wife was "adopted" into the man's family—thus women in the U.S. and much of Europe still today are likely to take their husband's surname. Women were even *abducted* for marriage, either in reality or ceremonially, thus the tradition of a husband carrying his bride over the threshold. Eventually, a different type of marriage emerged, one of greater mutuality if not complete equality. Nonetheless, Boswell asserts, "nothing in the ancient world quite corresponds to the idea of a permanent, exclusive union of social equals, freely chosen by them to fulfill both their emotional needs and imposing equal obligations of fidelity on both partners."[17]

Four Perspectives on Marriage

In *From Sacrament to Contract: Marriage, Religion and Law in the Western Tradition*, law and religion professor John Witte, Jr., delineates four complementary perspectives on marriage that evolved in Western Christian tradition: the religious, social, contractual, and naturalist perspectives. The religious perspective views marriage as spiritual, associated with the beliefs and community of the church. The social perspective considers marriage subject to the expectations of the community and the state. The contractual perspective emphasizes the choice of the individuals involved. And the naturalist perspective "treats marriage as a created institution, subject to the natural laws of reason, conscience, and the Bible."[18]

According to Witte, Roman Catholicism developed a sacramental model for marriage that brought together the natural, contractual, and religious aspects. The natural component included procreation, but also a way to limit lust and focus energy on the upbuilding of the church. Consent of the couple to enter marriage and to care for one another fulfilled the contractual element. Finally, marriage was emblematic of the marriage of Christ and the church, thus sacramental. "Marriage was more of a remedy for sin than a recipe for righteousness," Witte clarifies.[19] Those with religious vocation were now to abstain from marriage, and those within it were not to interfere with procreation because of marriage's God-given, naturalist characteristic. (Note that though the roots of this view can be found in earlier Christian writings, a more comprehensive embrace of marriage did not begin to emerge until the eleventh century, as stated earlier, and celibacy was still viewed as spiritually superior. And the prohibition of clergy from marriage was not absolute in earlier times.)

Protestants, emerging in the sixteenth century, also affirmed the naturalist and contractual elements of marriage, while rejecting its sacramental understanding as well as its subordination to celibacy. Protestants instead embraced the social perspective of marriage, recognizing it as a social institution that, like the church and state, was ordained by God. "Lutherans emphasized the social dimensions of marriage; Calvinists the covenantal dimensions; and Anglicans, the commonwealth dimensions. . . . Lutherans consigned legal authority mostly to the state; Calvinists to both the state and church; and Anglicans, mostly to the church," Witte explains.[20] Thus Lutherans established civil marriage courts. Calvinists emphasized marriage as a covenant among God, the community, and the couple. Anglicans viewed marriage as "a little commonwealth" that reflected the greater English commonwealth; as the latter became less authoritarian and more democratic, so did Anglican marriages.

The Enlightenment of the eighteenth century, according to Witte, emphasized the contractual understanding of marriage, and was neither fully nor legally implemented until the twentieth century, coming to full flower for the United States in the decades following the 1960s. In this view, marriage was essentially contractual, between the partners involved, and with no obligations to God, nature, church, state, tradition, or community, except to respect the "life, liberty, and property interests" of all parties and exercise "compliance with general standards of health, safety, and welfare in the community."[21] We see this philosophy of marriage manifest today in prenuptial arrangements, no-fault divorce laws, the diminishing if not absent need of parental consent and witnesses to the marriage, and an increasing emphasis on privacy and sexual autonomy. The state now watchdogs *nonconsensual* sexual activities more than *consensual* sexual relationships. However, Witte concludes this does not mean a secularization of marriage in that our present understanding of marital equality is "every bit as religious in inspiration as earlier Christian constructions of marital hierarchy."[22]

In my view, among the lessons to be taken from this historical analysis, which will be revisited in greater depth in Chapter Six, is that when states decriminalized adult consensual same-gender sexual relationships, they forfeited any legal claim of the superiority (or privileging) of opposite-gender sexual relationships. Now contractual elements of marriage may be applied equally to same-gender and opposite-gender partnerships. And the same religious inspiration that led to an affirmation of marital equality between partners in an opposite-gender marriage can lead to an affirmation of marital equality for same-gender marriages. To disqualify same-gender couples that fulfill these simple requirements for civil marriage in this era is to apply to them a different standard based on nostalgia for the way marriages used to be rather than on any civil, moral, or religious principle. Of course, churches (and other religious groups) may continue to deny *ecclesiastical* marriages, given their tendencies to be exclusive rather than inclusive—even if at odds with their Founder.

Variations on Marriage and Family Today

Not long ago, I was welcomed into a family's living room in a small town in Wisconsin. As I spoke with their parents, two tow-headed toddlers played at our feet on the living room floor. For all intents and purposes, this was a traditional family. The parents were biological parents of the children. Their uniqueness, however, lay in the fact that the parents were both women, and each had given birth, one to a boy, one to a girl, using the donated sperm of the partners of a gay couple who were close friends.

When people think "traditional family values" or "traditional marriage," we usually mean what's normative in our own experience or that of our parents or grandparents—or at least, what we *believe* to be normative, if not our actual experience. It is true that for some, "traditional family values" and "traditional marriage" have become catch phrases, even slogans, delimiting family to father, mother, and children, excluding models that do not fit this standard. "Traditional family values" has become a political rallying cry for conservative political action groups, such as the Rev. Lou Sheldon's "Traditional Values Coalition" or Dr. James Dobson's "Focus on the Family." Given the earlier sections of this chapter revisiting the historical variations on marriage, a fair question for those who campaign for traditional family values would be: how far back should we go in adopting "traditional" forms of marriage and family?

But many of us have a broader definition of family. Some families, for example, include "shirttail relatives," who are not related by blood or marriage, but treated as kin. Other families are headed by single parents. A friend who grew up in a single-parent home resisted outsiders referring to his family as a "broken home," because, though his mother and father had divorced and he was being raised by a single mother, he experienced his family as whole and complete.

Contemporary marriage, too, is not quite what we might expect. Based on census statistics and other research, Marvin Ellison points out ways that marriage differs from our "traditional" images in *Same-Sex Marriage? A Christian Ethical Analysis:*[23] First marriages last, on the average, eight years; second marriages, five to six years. One in four adults divorces. One in three marriages are remarriages. Marriage is not a requirement to have children, and having children is not the main reason for marriage. And, he writes, "Contrary to stereotype, evangelical and fundamentalist Christians divorce on average at a slightly higher rate than the rest of the population (30 percent and 27 percent respectively)."[24]

In modern times, the term "marriage" has come to be applied to a wide variety of relationships: life-long monogamous commitments, open relationships, serial monogamy (most common in the U.S.), common law couplings, abusive or codependent relationships, couples with children, couples without children, couples who never intend to have children, same-gender couples (in several countries and states), communal or polygamous arrangements, relationships that lack mutuality as well as those that enjoy mutuality, sexless as well as sexual relationships, unloving and loving couplings, single-race or mixed-race couples, mixed-faith couples, atheist couples, relationships of convenience (financially, or to fend off loneliness), couples living separately by choice or circumstance, "power" couples, murderous couples, criminal couples, couples unable to consummate the relationship (for example, where one is in prison, or if one has a prohibiting disability), couples with a sterile partner, and more. Perhaps the struggle of some to include same-gender couples within the rubric of "marriage" is, as Jonathan Rauch observes, simply a lack of imagination.

We may talk about an "ideal" of marriage, but few live it, and fewer demand it, at least of heterosexuals, in order to call it a marriage. Only when it comes to same-gender couples has the general public been more likely to "feel" marriage is threatened. Yet the model itself has been so abused by opposite-gender couplings that a 1991 Presbyterian task force on human sexuality proposed substituting a concept of "justice-love" as the paradigm for sexual ethics rather than marriage.[25] (Partly because it was misperceived as an "attack" on marriage, the report was not approved for study by the Presbyterian General Assembly, the legislative body of the Presbyterian Church, U.S.A. However, it is available in the minutes of said gathering!) Indeed, the arguments against same-gender marriage made by some Queer activists are more persuasive if based on the inequitable, unjust, and sometimes downright abusive models of marriage in history and the present time.[26]

A friend of mine postponed marriage for a very long time, not because he was not fully committed in love to his female partner, but because, he later told me, he had the notion that "marriage" was what his parents had, and he did not want their style of marriage, partly because of its inequities and codependencies. Finally he married when he realized that he and his wife could define marriage for themselves. Isn't this what's happening when couples today write their own wedding vows? Isn't this revealed as so many couples choose to wed outside houses of worship, like at the beach or a park or a club? Aren't they redefining marriage in a way that seems loving and just and honest, and practically applied to their own circumstances? Mutual consent, rather than procreation, is what made a marriage in the Roman empire, a model emulated by the early church, thus: "The teaching of the Roman church was ultimately, in part by default of a general ecclesiastical practice, that *the couple married each other*: the church at most witnessed and blessed (as it blessed everything from fields to swords)."[27] (Emphasis mine.) Could not a same-gender couple marry each other within this understanding of marriage? And, as one exasperated cleric once put it to me, "For God's sake, if we can bless animals and boats, buildings and homes, we can surely bless gay and lesbian couples!"

Can the elastic term "marriage" stretch to fit gay and lesbian partnerships? The present debate on the terminology elicits memories of my early years in the LGBT movement, especially when some people take offense and ask, "Can't they just take another term, like 'unions' or 'domestic partnerships'?" Thirty years ago, when the present LGBT movement was just beginning, there was controversy over "spoiling" the term "gay" for its other uses by applying it to homosexual persons. Notice that purity and taboo issues were at stake, in that the "impure" use of the term could spoil its "pure" use of "happy." I myself was never keen on the designation "gay," but I do believe in the right of a group to self-designation. Designated "Negroes" chose to be called "black" and now often but not always choose "African-American." The slogan "Black is beautiful" was an appropriate response to the imagined purity associated with "white." Depending on circumstance, adolescent and adult females may prefer to be called "women" rather than the diminutive "girls." "People living with HIV and AIDS" prefer that designation over "victims of AIDS" or even "AIDS patients." Even so, homosexual people have a right to self-designation, whether to be called gay or lesbian, or, among the more radical, to reclaim *faggot* and *queer* and *dyke*, just as "Christians" self-designated themselves with a term first used pejoratively. I believe we also have the right to self-designate our relationships.

I have just completed work on a curriculum for congregations about transgender people.[28] The most challenging segment considered the changing concepts and definitions for various life experiences within this emerging community. It was pointed out that using the right word and the right pronoun is essential, just like someone addressing us by our correct names. The reader might take a moment to consider how respected you feel when someone calls you by the right name, or gets your vocation right, or remembers an affiliation vital to your identity.

As a concept I believe that "marriage" is like "the sabbath." Just as Jesus declared that the institution of the sabbath was made for humanity, not humanity for the sabbath,[29] so marriage is made for us, not we for the institution of marriage. Like the sabbath, marriage serves as a vital, spiritual discipline to deepen our love for God and one another. And just as Christians "honor the sabbath" on Sunday while Jews honor it on Saturday, so marriage is honored by same-gender couples as well as opposite-gender couples. L. William Countryman explains that "the emphasis found in the Gospels [is] that laws exist to enhance a faithful human life, not place burdens on it."[30] Jesus made his declaration on the sabbath in the context of the question about when it is appropriate to demonstrate love and compassion, mercy and justice—our central means of loving and honoring God. *Every* day is such a time; even so, *every* marriage, regardless of the genders involved, is such an opportunity.

Further Variations on Family

We also have very different understandings of family than the ancients. Today "family" has warm and fuzzy connotations for many—though not all—of us. Its ideal is a mother and father and siblings who not only "*have* to take you in," but "*want* to take you in." In a perfect world, a family offers each member unconditional positive regard, though not license, because love "does not rejoice in wrongdoing, but rejoices in the truth" (1 Corinthians 13:6)—in other words, hoping all the best for the beloved.

But the word family is derived from the Latin *famulus*, which means *servant*, implying that a *paterfamilias* (father) owned and regulated all members of the household, including wife, children, relatives under his care, servants, and slaves—and this included sexual access to each of them.[31] This etiology amplifies the notion presented in the earlier discussion on marriage: the man had proprietorship—sexual and otherwise—not only of his wife or wives, but of the children and others of the household as well. Those who do not have warm and fuzzy connotations for the word "family" may have grown up in such a family, where the father ruled the roost, demanded unquestioning obedience of wife and children (even of adult children), and may have gone so far as to commit emotional, physical, spiritual, or sexual abuse. This would not be a happy family.

In reality, most families of ancient times probably fell somewhere between our Brady Bunch or Huxtable notions of family and a *pater-fascist* (my own word) notion. Nonetheless, this latter understanding was the default position on marriage—the bottom line, so to speak. Even today, religious fundamentalists of whatever religion may lean toward this concept of family (while at the same time, one hopes, condemning abuse), and yet simultaneously view and even experience themselves as the contemporary ideal of the happy family.

Another huge difference between today's families and those of the past is the one between the nuclear family common in the present and the extended family assumed in the past. Modern independence and mobility of husband, wife, and children does not make for a traditional family, at least not in biblical terms. A traditional family would have included a host of relations: grandparents, aunts, uncles, cousins, in-laws, and so on. As well as contributing to all aspects of family life, all family members would have been in some sense responsible for rearing children and assisting kin with disabilities, illness, or age-related limitations. More traditional are the extended families visible in some ethnic cultures today, as well as those within the LGBT community, whose couples frequently create an extended family of non-biological members, especially if biological family members are not accepting or nearby. Indeed, much as the early Christians came to view themselves as an extended family regardless of blood ties, sharing possessions in common, addressing one another as brother and sister, the LGBT community considers itself a family of the whole, especially in the absence of welcoming biological or church families.

As an example, I enjoy telling the story of a straight clergy ally who had a flat tire driving me to a speaking engagement in rural Florida. He had his car towed to a mechanic's shop and left it in the hands of a bearded bear of a man in greasy overalls, wondering and worrying if the man would know the significance of the tiny rainbow windsock that hung from the rearview mirror, made of the six colors of the LGBT rainbow flag. Later, upon returning to pay for the repaired flat, the "redneck" said, gesturing toward the windsock, "No charge for family."[32] Small wonder that the Sister Sledge disco hit, "We Are Family," became an unofficial theme song of the LGBT movement!

Jesus on Family

Jesus' earthly parents never consummated their relationship, according to Roman Catholic doctrine. Protestants, of course, believe that there is evidence of a sexual relationship between Joseph and Mary in the brothers and sisters that Jesus was said to have had, the most prominent being James, the brother of Jesus, who headed the church at Jerusalem. Regardless of these differing points of view, both traditions hold that Joseph and Mary were merely betrothed at the time of Jesus' birth, which could mean that they lived together, and could include sexual intercourse, but did not according to the story, given the special nature of Mary's pregnancy. Jesus was therefore born to an unwed mother. None of this fits "traditional family values" as they are presented by many in our time.

As a child, Jesus disregarded his parents' concerns when he sojourned in the temple, being "about [his] Father's interest" (the alternative reading in the NRSV), apparently failing to tell them where he was. They noticed his absence after three days' journey from attending the Passover festivals in Jerusalem (an intended parallel perhaps to his three days in the grave after the Passover festival at the end of his life), testimony not to their neglect but to the presumed watchful care of their extended family. Though he was said subsequently to have "increased in wisdom and in years [or stature], and in divine and human favor" (Luke 2:52), his mother at the time seemed to reproach him for failing to keep the third commandment about honoring his father and mother, "Child, why have you treated us like this? Look, your father and I have been searching for you in great anxiety" (Luke 2:48). A precocious child, even then he knew that his calling mitigated traditional regard for family.

As far as the biblical account informs us, Jesus never married, though his possible celibacy did not diminish his regard for the sensual joys of marriage, evidenced by his turning baptismal water set aside for purification rituals (thus transforming external signs of purity) into a fine wine during the several-day-long wedding feast at Cana (John 3). Not only did Jesus attend the feast, but his first miracle involved a celebration of the senses, turning the ordinary means of fulfilling ritual obligation into an extraordinary means of pleasuring the palate and body, and lightening the soul.

Again, his possible celibacy did not prevent him from intimacy, not as a euphemism for sexuality, but as another intimacy of soul with soul and body with body, exampled by his close relationship with Mary Magdalene (to whom he first revealed his resurrected body) and the Beloved Disciple (who lay on his breast during the Last Supper, though subsequent translations keep coming between them, removing the physical intimacy found in the actual Greek text), his request of a drink of water from the Samaritan woman at the well, his desire to welcome children into his arms, and his gracious acceptance of the ministrations of a disreputable woman who washed his feet with her tears, dried them with her hair, and continually kissed them. This is a celibacy that nonetheless welcomes the soulful and sacred intimacy possible when bodies touch.

And Jesus touched every body, from lepers to blind or deaf men, on his own initiative or through the initiative of people of faith, such as the woman with a hemorrhage, who touched *him*. Jesus was the ultimate spiritual leader in terms of accessibility. His respect for bodily life was represented by his resurrection of Lazarus, whose sister Mary had been described as the one who anointed Jesus' body with a precious nard, the perfume of which filled the room. His Father God had hallowed bodily existence, not by simply shaping the body of the first human creatures with his own hands, but wrestling into the body of Christ in the Incarnation, and finally, by resurrecting Jesus' body from the dead, replete with the wounds that killed him. As such, Jesus becomes the wounded healer that rabbis described as the very nature of Messiah. And our memory of him is our own death and resurrection through the tangible waters of baptism and the transformation of his blood to wine and his body to bread that tastefully fosters spiritual ecstasy and physical preservation.

How we got to a pyramid of control that separates God from human experience and spirit from body as described in the previous chapter is one of the great theological misdirections. For God and Jesus are all about the body and the earth and the soul—the indivisible unit of spirit and body that ancient Hebrews and early Christians recognized as sacred and eternal. And the Holy Spirit was sent to keep us mindful of that integrity, that atonement effected between God and humanity in Jesus Christ.

Given his overriding concern to proclaim the gospel of God's commonwealth, the forgiveness of sins, and the inclusive nature of God's grace, Jesus clearly has higher priorities than marriage, procreation, and family. There are spiritual friendships, Christian siblings, the family of those who do the will of God in heaven. How difficult it must have been for Jesus' family to hear him say, when they came to see him, "'Who is my mother, and who are my brothers?' And pointing to his disciples, [Jesus] said, 'Here are my mother and my brothers! For whoever does the will of my Father in heaven is my brother and sister and mother'"(Matthew 12:48b–50). Probably this was no more painful than it was when Jesus called his disciples away from their families to follow him. The family of faith would now have ascendancy over the biological family. Even from the cross, Jesus called his beloved disciple and his most holy mother to be family for one another.

And yet there's more. "Whoever comes to me and does not hate father and mother, wife and children, brothers and sisters, yes, and even life itself, cannot be my disciples," Jesus declared (Luke 14:26). Jesus' language of Aramaic did not have superlatives like "more" and "most"—thus this seemingly harsh saying, but even so, his priorities are clear. To the man who wants to delay his discipleship until after he has taken care of family responsibilities, waiting until his father is dead, Jesus bluntly demands, "Follow me, and let the dead bury their own dead" (Matthew 8:22). To the rich man who, having fulfilled the Law, asks what more he should do to inherit eternal life, Jesus advises to sell his possessions, redistributing the money to the poor and effectively disinheriting his family (Mark 10:17–22). A few verses later Jesus explains to Peter, "Truly I tell you, there is no one who has left house or brothers or sisters or mother or father or children or fields, for my sake and for the sake of the good news [gospel], who will not receive a hundredfold now in this age . . . and in the age to come eternal life" (Mark 10:29–30).

Jesus appears more threatening to marriage and family than same-gender marriage and LGBT people, who appear rather to reinforce the value of these venerable institutions by wanting them. Yet only *same-gender* marriages and families are threatened by most of Jesus' *present followers*, something of which he does not speak. "Deny your love, your lover, your family, and follow me," opponents and even moderate Christians might imagine Jesus saying to gay Christians, while ignoring or setting aside Jesus' strong rhetoric that might at the least "decenter" marriage, heterosexuality, and biological family as privileged statuses.

"What would it mean *to decenter marriage* and not grant it privileged status?" Christian ethicist Marvin Ellison wonders in his prescient 2004 book *Same-Sex Marriage?* "What would it mean *to decenter heterosexuality* and not grant it privileged status? What would a progressive Christian ethic look like that regarded homosexuality as a morally good way to be and 'do' sexuality? What difference would it make to focus moral concern not on gender and sexual identity, but on the quality of relational intimacy and whether our connections with one another are just and compassionate?"[33] To put it in the terms of the sexuality task force mentioned earlier, on which Ellison served, what would happen if we substituted "justice-love" as the goal of sexual relationships rather than "opposite-gender marriage"? As Ellison concludes, "Paradoxically, conservatives undermine their own case for marriage as a fixed, unalterable institution insofar as they insist, on the one hand, that the patriarchal family is natural and, on the other hand, that it requires special privileging in order to survive."[34]

In his book, *Gay Marriage: Why It Is Good for Gays, Good for Straights, and Good for America*, conservative journalist Jonathan Rauch takes things a step further, persuasively arguing that alternatives to marriage for gay couples, such as domestic partnerships, civil unions, and simple cohabitation—what Rauch humorously calls "marriage lite"—effectively weaken marriage by serving as attractive and less demanding alternatives for opposite-gender couples as well, who have insisted businesses and governments give them the same opportunities for arrangements that fall short of all the responsibilities of marriage and yet reap many of the same benefits. By contrast, same-gender marriage would bolster the prominence and foster the respect of marriage on the whole.

Jesus and Chastity

Jesus was not necessarily anticipating our present debate (or is that a fair assumption of one we trust as Lord of the universe?). Ultimately, Jesus' view of the biological family could be said to be based on chastity, which is not celibacy, not the cessation of sexual expression, but the *subordination of desire to responsibility*,[35] his purity of heart and purity of purpose to manifest and proclaim the love and grace of the inbreaking commonwealth of God. This is what prompted Jesus to leave his own family and call the disciples to leave theirs. This is what caused Paul to be single and recommend the same for others. In his book *The Four Loves*, C. S. Lewis doubts that the New Testament concern about marriage has to do with sexuality, but rather, "the multiple distractions of domesticity. It is marriage itself, not the marriage bed, that will be likely to hinder us from waiting uninterruptedly on God. . . . The gnat-like cloud of petty anxieties and decisions about the conduct of the next hour have interfered with my prayers more often than any passion or appetite whatever."[36]

The closet is a perfect example of how much and how often gay people have subordinated desire to responsibility. Trying to do the best we can, many of us hid or hide our sexuality in a closet. Many of us prayed for change, another attempt to subordinate our desire to what we were taught was our responsibility as Christians. What brought many of us out of the closet was not our sexual desire, but our desire to be responsible, to be honest, to seek a public relationship. One can always have sex from the safety of the closet; but to have a marriage requires a degree of public disclosure, of accountability, and at the least, a semblance of community. As Mel White, the founder of Soulforce, explains in the 2007 film, *For the Bible Tells Me So*, in the closet "you're cut off from all that confessing, all of that conversation, all of that inter-play with others that makes you healthy."

The leader of a group in my denomination opposed to gay and lesbian ministers and marriages once asked me if I would be willing "to change" if led by the Spirit. To this absurd hypothetical, I replied that I knew of no group of people who had been *more* willing to change than gay people, as most of us grew up hoping and praying to be like those in the majority culture. But I pointed out of his own anti-gay constituency that I knew of no group that seemed *less* willing to change, to subordinate their desire to exclude us to their responsibility to be compassionate and fair and welcoming as Jesus. And, as discussed in the previous chapter, learned behavior is changeable as sexual orientation is not. To his credit, my opponent "got it," though it didn't change his view.

Jesus' primary message was that "the kingdom of God is at hand." Thus Jesus' strong rhetoric on family could be understood as having to do with the claims of the inbreaking commonwealth of God, which affected the claims of every relationship: marital, family, or otherwise. Desire must be subordinated to the new reality, as "new occasions teach new duties." Men could no longer have the privilege of divorce (Matthew 5: 31–32; as well as 19:9). Nor could they feel spiritually superior because they "only" lusted in their hearts (Matthew 5:27–28). Nor was it legitimate to dedicate to God finances that would have taken care of parents, with no further obligation to honor them with financial support (Mark 7:9–13). Scapegoating a woman for men's sexual misbehavior was unacceptable (John 8:7). Marriage was not eternal, but life was (Matthew 21:23–30). Family members could not be trusted (Matthew 10:34–36).

In positive contrast, Jesus entrusted his mission and message to a Samaritan woman who had to come to the town well in the middle of the day rather than in the morning with the other women, possibly out of shame; one who had had five men or husbands and lived with another. She became the first Christian evangelist (John 4:7–42). Children who had little or no status in the family or society were to be welcomed and would be first in the kingdom of heaven (Mark 10:13–16). Publicly admiring his great faith, Jesus was willing to heal the Gentile centurion's *pais* or "adopted son or brother," a common practice of ancient same-gender couples (Luke 7:1–10).[37] And, Jesus said, sex workers will enter the kingdom of God ahead of chief priests and elders (Matthew 21:31).

One of the most radical parables Jesus told was that of the Prodigal. To modern ears, it is a sweet little story of parental forgiveness as metaphor for God's forgiveness; but it would have burned in the ears of his pro-family contemporaries. In Jesus' culture, for a son to leave home, asking for his portion of the inheritance, was essentially to say to the father, "You're dead to me!" In *The Return of the Prodigal Son*, Henri Nouwen describes the devastation, grief, and anger such an action would elicit. It would have been the ultimate way of dishonoring parents and their values. Further, leaving for a distant country was the absolute rejection of the values of the prodigal's culture and community.[38]

Jesus' listeners would have been shocked and horrified and unforgiving. The *son* would have been dead to them! Yet the story is ultimately about the aggressive forgiveness of the father, aggressive in his running down the road to welcome his bedraggled son and in his having no need to hear the son's apology before restoring him to his position in the family, with robe and ring and sandals—symbols, respectively, of authority and belonging and sonship. The father's actions might have been as offensive and unreasonable to Jesus' listeners as it was to the elder brother who refused to celebrate the prodigal's return and with whom Pharisees (read: good people of Jesus' time) would have likely identified.

The traditional family values of Jesus' time were turned inside out by the extravagant, excessive, and aggressive grace and love of God, who, like the father in the parable, wants both elder brother and prodigal to share table fellowship, regardless. Confession is not even required, just coming home.

Jesus on Marriage and Procreation

During an interview about LGBT people and the church on a local public radio station in Champaign-Urbana, Illinois, the host mentioned I'd be preaching the next day at a local church. Sunday morning, church members discovered a sign affixed to the church's front door, apparently meant to protest my presence. It simply cited the biblical reference "Matthew 19:3–12," which is Jesus' teaching on divorce and, by implication, marriage. The ironic twist was that the reference was what I had earlier chosen as the text for my sermon that day!

Part of the wealth of the Bible is that each passage may be read in diverse ways. Anyone who regularly uses scripture as a source of meditation has discovered that reading the same text at different points of our lives may offer very different meanings. The previous chapter suggested that taking the Bible seriously involves being mindful of our own presuppositions; utilization of insight provided by scholars and the church of times past; letting scripture interpret scripture through comparisons; relying on the Holy Spirit as we meditate on its meaning for us; and opening our interpretations to challenge or confirmation from our spiritual community. I might only guess at the interpretation of Matthew 19:3–12 by the person leaving the sign on the church door; but apparently he or she thought it was clear. And whatever his or her "clear" interpretation was, it needed to be stated, and then evaluated by the spiritual community of that congregation.

My own interpretation was presented to the church that morning. Religious leaders sought "to test" Jesus by asking him about divorce. Jesus responds with the Genesis passage about God creating males and females, and how they become one flesh in marriage. "Therefore," Jesus concludes, "What God has joined together, let no one separate." But what about Moses allowing for divorce, they question (the certificate of dismissal mentioned earlier). Jesus explains it was because of the hardheartedness of men, parrying, "And I say to you, whoever divorces his wife, except for unchastity, and marries another commits adultery." Remember, unchastity would be the failure to subordinate desire to responsibility, and the implication here is the subordination of sexual desire to marital responsibility, though just about any desire of the woman had to be subjugated to her marital responsibility in a marriage of that time and place.

As I read it, there is nothing about homosexuality in this portion of the text. There is, however, an unequivocal prohibition of divorce from none other than Jesus himself. Divorce breaks apart what God has joined, not homosexuality. Divorce will lead to adultery if either remarries, though here Jesus mentions only the man, at least in the Greek manuscript used by the NRSV. In an example of scriptural comparisons, Matthew 5:31–32 indicates that the man would cause the divorced woman, too, to commit adultery. Again, nothing about homosexuality. Heterosexuals do divorce and adultery all by themselves.

I suppose my closeted opponent who tacked his protest scripture to the church door thought that in this text Jesus declared opposite-gender marriage as the only one that God makes one flesh. Before addressing this interpretation, I would like to point out that self-designated "conservatives" often are the most "liberal" when interpreting a text; that is, they sometimes read more into a scripture than may be intended. Reading one's bias into a text is called *eisegesis* (*eis*=into) as opposed to *exegesis* (*ex*=out of), letting the text speak for itself. Another example is the story of Adam and Eve mentioned earlier: self-designated "conservatives" read an exclusion of same-gender couples into a text never intended to address the question of homosexuality.

In the scripture from Matthew, Jesus' primary concern seems to be divorce, and, looking deeper, he appears particularly critical of men's "hardheartedness" in relation to women. Given Jesus' sensitivity to the plight and worth of women overall, it sounds very much like he's taking on men who disrespected the spiritual union of marriage as well as their wives. Further, given Jesus' attitude toward lawful obligations, such as not working on the sabbath, one might wonder if Jesus is not here defending women rather than the institution of marriage itself.

Even if the historical Jesus were defending marriage as an institution, much of the church has subsequently set aside his teaching on divorce on similar grounds of pastoral compassion that caused Jesus to set aside the institution of the sabbath in certain circumstances, whether simply feeding his hungry disciples or healing strangers. But so far in this Matthean text, no homosexual person has been the cause of upsetting God's will for humanity.

However, when Jesus' disciples question his strong criticism of divorce, Jesus essentially replies, "One saying doesn't fit all": "Not everyone can accept this teaching, but only those to whom it is given. For there are eunuchs who have been so from birth, and there are eunuchs who have been made eunuchs by others, and there are eunuchs who have made themselves eunuchs for the sake of the kingdom of heaven. Let anyone accept this who can."

Some interpreters of this text suggest that here Jesus is striking a blow for celibacy, but again, that's reading a bias for celibacy into the text. And celibacy is considered by the church a spiritual charism, or gift, not a product of one's physiognomy. (Remember it is chastity, not celibacy, that is emphasized in proclaiming the gospel.) So why does he talk about eunuchs in the context of marriage and divorce? Given his compassion for outcasts, this could be just one more category of those on the outside—first, because their bodies had been maimed or scarred (another Hebrew taboo), and second, and perhaps more importantly, because they could not procreate, a virtual sin in Israel. It has even been argued that the term eunuch served as a euphemism for a gay man in the ancient world,[39] but to apply that understanding here may also be reading too much into this particular text.

The prophet Isaiah had spoken out for eunuchs in Isaiah 56, a text familiar to Jesus because he quoted Isaiah 56:7 when he overturned the tables of the merchants who helped worshipers fulfill their ritual obligations in the temple. Later, in Acts 8, the Spirit would lead Philip to an Ethiopian eunuch reading—coincidentally?—the prophet Isaiah. After Philip interpreted the scripture to him, the eunuch asked to be baptized on the spot. As I concluded in my second book, *Come Home!*:

> These passages taken together suggest we pay close attention to Jesus' reference to eunuchs in Matthew's Gospel. Jesus tells his disciples that the teaching on heterosexual marriage—that a man shall cleave to his wife and become one flesh—doesn't apply to eunuchs, who have been so from birth, have been made so by others, or who have made themselves so. This covers all ways possible for someone to be gay, lesbian, or bisexual, doesn't it? Born that way (which I believe to be the case), made that way by environment (which some people believe), or consciously chosen (which some gay leaders claim to be most politically correct and which many of our opponents claim to suggest how perverse we are). But more importantly, whether by nature, nurture, or decision, Jesus implies that a citizen of God's kingdom or commonwealth does not have to procreate.
>
> This is because, in Christian scripture, the biological, polygamous, prolifically procreative family gives way to the more vital, important, and eternal family of faith, a family to be expanded by evangelism and inclusivity rather than by simple procreation.[40]

Notes

[1] Boswell, *Same-Sex Unions in Premodern Europe*, 111.

[2] Rauch, *Gay Marriage*, 40–41.

[3] Stephanie Coontz, *Marriage, a History: How Love Conquered Marriage* (New York: Penguin Books, 2006), 83.

[4] Rabbi Elliot Rose Kukla, "How I Met the Tumtum," in *Gender Identity and Our Faith Communities: A Congregational Guide Toward Transgender Advocacy,* ed. Chris Glaser (Washington, DC, 2008: Human Rights Campaign), online resource available at *http://www.hrc.org/* (accessed March 27, 2009).

[5] Boswell, *Same-Sex Unions in Premodern Europe*, 58–59; Bernadette Brooten, *Love Between Women: Early Christian Responses to Female Homoeroticism* (Chicago: University of Chicago Press, 1996), 41.

[6] Boswell, *Same-Sex Unions*, 60.

[7] Boswell, *Same-Sex Unions*, 61.

[8] Brooten, *Love Between Women,* 107.

[9] Coontz, *Marriage, a History,* 77.

[10] Boswell, *Same-Sex Unions*, 74.

[11] *The New Oxford Annotated Bible*, NRSV (New York: Oxford University Press, 1991), 391 OT, commentary on 2 Samuel 5:13–16.

[12] Coontz, *Marriage, a History*.

[13] Boswell, *Same-Sex Unions*, 35.

[14] *The HarperCollins Bible Dictionary*, Paul J. Achtemeier, editor (San Francisco: HarperSanFrancisco, 1996), "Marriage," 656–657.

[15] Bernadette Brooten, "The Bible and Love Between Women," *Open Hands*, Vol. 15, No. 4 (Winter 2000), 15.

[16] Rauch, *Gay Marraiges,* 41.

[17] Boswell, *Same-Sex Unions*, 38.

[18] Witte, *From Sacrament to Contract,* 2.

[19] Witte, 4.

[20] Witte, 5.

[21] Witte, 10.

[22] Witte, 12.

[23] Ellison, *Same-Sex Marriage?*, 16.

[24] Ellison, 16.

[25] The Special Committee on Human Sexuality, *Keeping Body and Soul Together: Sexuality, Spirituality, and Social Justice, Presbyterians and Human Sexuality 1991* (Louisville, KY: The Presbyterian Church (U.S.A.), 1991).

[26] Ellison, *Same-Sex Marriage?*, Chapter Five, "Marriage Critics."

[27] Boswell, *Same-Sex Unions*, 165.

[28] *Gender Identity and Our Faith Communities: A Congregational Guide Toward Transgender Advocacy*, ed. Chris Glaser (Washington, DC: Human Rights Campaign, 2008), available as on online resource at *www.hrc.org* (accessed March 27, 2009).

[29] Mark 2:23–3:6, specifically 2:27.

[30] L. William Countryman, *Dirt, Greed, and Sex: Sexual Ethics in the New Testament and Their Implications for Today* (Philadelphia: Fortress Press, 1988), 210.

[31] Boswell, *Same-Sex Unions*, 40.

[32] Harold Brockus, "We're Family," *Open Hands*, Vol. 16, No. 4 (Spring 2001), 6.

[33] Ellison, *Same-Sex Marriage?*, 5.

[34] Ellison, 69.

[35] Boswell, *Same-Sex Unions*, 24.

[36] C.S. Lewis, *Readings for Meditation and Reflection*, ed. Walter Hooper (San Francisco: HarperSanFrancisco, 1992), 119.

[37] Thomas C. Ziegert, "Blessed and Challenged by Jesus: Where We Get the Chutzpah to Do Our Own Ethics," *Open Hands*, Vol. 13, No. 4 (Spring 1998), 14.

[38] Henri J. M. Nouwen, *The Return of the Prodigal Son* (New York: Continuum, 1995), 31–33.

[39] Nancy Wilson, in her book, *Our Tribe: Queer Folks, God, Jesus, and the Bible* (San Francisco: HarperSanFrancisco, 1995; revised, briefer Millennium Edition: Tajique, NM: Alamo Square Press, 2000), explains that "eunuch" could also simply mean a government official or a gay man, not necessarily castrated.

[40] Chris Glaser, *Come Home! Reclaiming Spirituality and Community as Gay Men and Lesbians*, second edition (Gaithersburg, MD: Chi Rho Press, 1998), 118–119.

CHAPTER FOUR

The Sacred Source of Marriage

Holy Origins and Sacramental Dimensions

"It is not good that the man should be alone . . ."
God in Genesis 2:18

"What God has joined together, let no one separate."
Jesus in Matthew 19:6

I attended a talk and book signing by Jonathan Rauch, a correspondent for the *Atlantic Monthly*, a senior writer and columnist for the *National Journal*, and a writer in residence at the Brookings Institution. His book, *Gay Marriage*, referenced earlier, presents a tightly reasoned argument in favor of same-gender marriage that is secular in its approach. Those gathered for his presentation at Atlanta's Outwrite Bookstore were a mix of black and white patrons, primarily gay and lesbian, and all supportive of the concept of marriage, especially two men, active in the Episcopal church, who had recently celebrated their golden anniversary. During the question-and-answer period after his talk, Rauch was asked what, in his view, was the biggest obstacle to the acceptance of same-gender marriage. His opinion was that the greatest reservation people have is marriage's association with a sacred source, with God, even among those who are not particularly religious.

This is as it should be. The taboo that must give us pause should not be a negative one relating to purity laws or human custom; it must be the positive taboo associated with what is sacred, holy, of God. Our contemporary beliefs have sometimes domesticated God, or boxed God into particular theological corners. If only we could return to the day when *theologia* meant active mystical communing with God in prayer rather than the systematization of God in religious doctrine and dogma! Perhaps then we could better be awed and inspired by the God who runs deeper than human imagination, experience, reason, and ability to either comprehend or name. Moderate and mainstream Christians tend toward a "gentleman God," as I once heard Carter Heyward describe him, a sometimes passionless but always polite deity, not willing, for example, to exclude LGBT people, but too dispassionate to stand up for our rights, perhaps even embarrassed by our sexual passion. Conservative Christians may emphasize a terrifying God of judgment. Progressive Christians may emphasize a God of Justice, which remarkably, can have the same edge of judgment as that of conservative Christians. Sentimentalist Christians may image God as a buddy, enjoying a self-assured "just-me-and-Jesus" spirituality. Evangelical Christians may emphasize a "good cop, bad cop" understanding of God, in which the God of judgment (bad cop) may be avoided by confession and conversion in the arms of Jesus, the "good cop." None of these views are necessarily incorrect, just perhaps incomplete.

It's when religious people get stuck on their particular metaphor for God, Joseph Campbell said, that problems arise. God must have shared the opinion, for the second commandment forbids graven images. God is behind, beyond, beneath any metaphor or image. Jack Rogers writes, "Calvin was bold to say we do not know God 'as he is in himself, but as he seems to us.' This attitude reflected Isaiah's reminder that God's thoughts are not our thoughts, nor are God's ways our ways (Isaiah 55:8)."[1] Annie Dillard has written that she wonders if churchgoers would so easily and frequently invoke God if they truly understood how terrifying it would be to stand in the actual presence of the awesome Lord of the universe. And Reformed theologian Karl Barth characterized the theologian's task as that of an artist trying to capture on canvas a bird in flight—by the time the painting is complete, the bird is elsewhere. A part of God's holiness is God's elusiveness, God's mystery. As mentioned earlier, "holy" means to be "set apart," and there is nothing more *set apart* than God—not in terms of distance, I believe, but in terms of uniqueness and expansiveness.

God as Taboo

The God of the Bible is at once an awesome and intimate God, one who cannot be known except through revelation and yet knows us completely from the moment we were knit together in our mother's womb, One who resides at the heart of the universe and yet within our own hearts as well, One who calls all into being through a Word of power and might and yet speaks to us in a still small voice. Moses, drawn to a bush that burned and yet was not consumed, was told to remove his sandals in reverence. Moses asked for God's name, which in the ancient view, would have given him a handle on God, a means of control. God answers evasively, "I am what I am" or "I will be what I will be," depending on translation, but, in either case, suggesting we can hold onto God no more than Mary Magdalene could cling to the risen Jesus. Consequently, Jewish tradition would not permit pronouncing Yahweh's name when scripture was read aloud, so *Adonai*, "Lord," was substituted.

After the exodus, Moses would lead his people back to Mount Sinai, where he had witnessed the burning bush. The mountain was taboo, holy, because God made God's presence known there. God demanded of Moses, "You shall set limits for the people all around, saying, 'Be careful not to go up the mountain or to touch the edge of it. Any who touch the mountain shall be put to death" (Exodus 19:12). "Set limits around the mountain and keep it holy" (19:23). "There was thunder and lightning, as well as a thick cloud on the mountain, and a blast of a trumpet so loud that all the people who were in the camp trembled" (Exodus 19:16). Only Moses and Aaron were invited to ascend the mountain, and when Moses asked to see God's face, God replied that no one could see God's face and live, but holding a hand in front of Moses' face as he passed by, Moses was given the opportunity to see God's backside, a kind of afterglow, if you will. Nonetheless the glow on Moses' face from this brief encounter was so terrible the people prevailed upon him to veil his face until the glow subsided. The Ten Commandments would be carried in the Ark of the Covenant, which would also be taboo, untouchable, on pain of death.

Jesus revealed quite another face of God, a more vulnerable and accessible one, one who could be touched and would touch, but nonetheless awesome, as the Gospels claim: he spoke with authority; he addressed God with the familiar form of Father (and encouraged us to do so in the Lord's Prayer); God's voice called him the Beloved Son; he resisted temptation and the Tempter and did not sin; he healed the sick and raised the dead; he was born of a virgin, with signs in the heavens and the magi of a foreign religion coming to pay him homage; he spoke with Moses and Elijah on a mountaintop and glowed from the experience, again hearing God's voice of approval; he rebuked not only the wind and rain on the Sea of Galilee but also "the powers that be" in the temple and city of Jerusalem—the religious and political authorities; he staged an angry and dramatic protest in the temple; he voluntarily died an excruciating death to complete at-one-ment of God and humanity; God resurrected him; he ascended to God, and sent his disciples the power of the Holy Spirit as a paraclete, an advocate for victims. At his death the temple curtain veiling the Holy of Holies was torn in two from top to bottom, from heaven to earth, giving us access to the holy in a new way. We too glow from our encounter with Jesus, but, unlike Moses, we are to do so with unveiled faces, as Paul wrote, so we may, by looking to one another, grow from glory unto glory. A tiny fraction of a fraction of a single percentage point of the population of the Roman Empire, Jesus' followers grew to encompass that empire in only four centuries. Jesus was truly awesome, yet completely accessible, "God with us," God become human, God's Word made flesh, full of grace and truth.

Comprehending the Sacred, Here and Now

It is through the life, teachings, and example of Jesus that Christians are to understand everything holy. The sacraments, whether the two of

Protestants or the seven of the Roman Catholic and Eastern Orthodox churches, were believed instituted by Jesus during his lifetime. (The difference in number is because Protestants recognize only those specified by Jesus.) That the Eastern Orthodox churches termed them "mysteries" suggests their unknowable sacred dimension. At one time, Christians observed as many as 150 sacraments, observing the sacred in almost every human activity. Seven were chosen to represent the whole, seven serving as a holy number symbolizing completeness.

I believe that Celtic Christianity best represents this understanding of the intimate interweaving of the sacred and the secular, the spiritual and the material, body and spirit, sexuality and spirituality, heaven and earth, time and eternity—all symbolized by the interweaving threads of Celtic crosses and other Celtic symbols. Though they came to be primarily associated with the British Isles, the Celts once stretched across Europe to Asia Minor. The holy was understood as in our midst, much as Jesus proclaimed the commonwealth of God among us. Portals to heaven were everywhere, "thin places" where the earthly may glimpse the heavenly. As a result, "The Celtic Church neither totally separated the sexes nor displayed the fear of sexuality that was to dominate much of the Western Church. As in Eastern Orthodoxy there were married priests and celibate monks, but the ecclesiastic leadership of women . . . was peculiar to the Celtic Church."[2]

Church of Scotland minister J. Philip Newell has documented Celtic Christian history in several books, including *Listening for the Heartbeat of God: A Celtic Spirituality*. The Celtic mission in Britain contrasted with that associated in Europe with the Bishop of Rome (not yet the pope), which took up Augustine of Hippo's concept of human depravity, adopted celibacy for priests, and widened the separation between God and humanity, heaven and earth, male and female, lay and clergy. The Celtic view did not distinguish as strongly between those with a religious vocation and laypeople, nor did it differentiate in a derogatory way between those inside or outside the church: all were made in the image of God. (Imagine how such an attitude would improve evangelism and mission, as well as international relations!) The Celtic view would have been the answer, or at least the balance, to James B. Nelson's pyramid of control presented earlier, if it had not been superseded by the Roman mission at the Synod of Whitby in 664 and almost obliterated by the Scottish Reformation. The latter emphasized the Augustinian–Calvinistic notion of human depravity and led to further separation between spirit and matter, the sacred and the secular.

This "holier than thou" approach may limit our comprehension of the holy even within the sacraments themselves. As Henri Nouwen observed, "We will never fully understand the meaning of the sacramental signs of bread and wine when they do not make us realize that the whole of nature is a sacrament pointing to a reality far beyond itself. The presence of Christ in the Eucharist becomes a 'special problem' only when we have lost our sense of God's presence in all that is, grows, lives, and dies."[3]

Nature as a Sacred Source

Ironically, though the church might eschew nature as sacred, it nonetheless served as an *imagined* source of natural law. Today people who are not religious may rely on nature and the natural as a sacred source, the way things were meant to be "from time immemorial"— an incantation of a kind of natural deity of the status quo. Perhaps the Amish are the only segment of present American society who at least attempt to live that out, as few others live "according to nature" when they watch TV, ride in cars, fly in planes, eat packaged and processed food, utilize contraception or *in vitro* fertilization, use the Internet, etc.

Christians, too, use nature as a sacred reference point. Our physiology points to male–female compatibility, goes one argument. The survival of any species requires procreation, goes another argument, bolstered by God's admonition in Genesis, "Be fruitful and multiply." When the AIDS crisis began, a cartoonist offensively depicted Mother Nature pointing accusingly toward two emaciated men with AIDS in hospital beds, parodying a margarine commercial of the time, "It's not nice to fool Mother Nature!" Yet Christians should not feel beholden to a pagan God, *Natura*, borrowed as a literary device of the late Middle Ages.

In its best sense, nature should serve as an epiphany of God, not as a model of human behavior. "The world is charged with the grandeur of God," Catholic priest and British poet Gerard Manley Hopkins celebrated, even as he practiced chastity, subordinating his homoerotic yearnings to his priestly work. Celtic Christianity held that Christ walked among us in two shoes, one being the Bible and the other being Creation. There are biblical antecedents to this way of thinking. Surely the wilderness in which the Israelites wandered shaped their understanding of God, as the wilderness in which Jesus fasted and prayed for forty days forged his earthly relationship with the Father. The Psalmists saw the wonder of God in nature, from our being "awesomely, wonderfully made" to the amazing wonders of the heavens, earth, and seas. Many of Jesus' spiritual metaphors came from nature, from the faith of a tiny mustard seed to the providence of God manifest in the lilies of the field and the birds of the air.

The apostle Paul, in his letter to the Romans discussed in an earlier chapter, thought Gentiles could have recognized the Creator in the creation, yet they acted "contrary to nature" in their exchange of "natural intercourse" for "shameless acts." In *Christianity, Social Tolerance, and Homosexuality: Gay People in Western Europe from the Beginning of the Christian Era to the Fourteenth Century,* John Boswell persuasively argues that Paul is simply speaking of them acting contrary to their personal natures. Acting "contrary to nature," is not of itself sinful or evil to Paul, Boswell argues, or he would not have used the exact same phrase (*para physin*) a few chapters later to describe God's action of grafting the Gentiles onto "the root of Jesse," the Jewish race. Indeed, the whole notion that Gentiles were now heirs of Abraham and Sarah is unnatural, i.e., not biologically or physiologically possible. Paul's basis for ethics was based on belonging to Christ, as will be discussed in the chapter that follows, not nature or the natural world.

Absent the evidence to the contrary of today's findings of cross-cultural researchers, late Roman thinkers considered that, across the laws of various nations, there were instinctual or natural laws, in other words, "the way things should be." But it was not until the High Middle Ages that people began to look to animals for cues on human behavior, partly caused by an increasingly urbanized population that idealized nature, and by mistaken empirical zoological observations. The Christian reader might readily see the dangers and contradictions inherent in appealing to nature for any kind of moral law. For example, the humane treatment of animals is not "natural": we can easily cite the common example of a cat playing with a mouse. The celibacy and virginity that was so highly valued for so much of Christian history (and still is in Roman Catholicism) is not the way they do it on *Animal Planet*. And today, most Christians no longer consider masturbation as unnatural, just as we no longer believe the use of contraceptive devices that interfere with procreation, a natural purpose of human sexuality, are immoral (though the Vatican officially does, but those "who know so little about marriage" have not persuaded the majority of American Catholics). And we know now that homosexual behavior is observable in other species.

The pinnacle of natural law was reached in the thirteenth century in the writings of Thomas Aquinas, commanding an influence in Roman Catholic sexual ethics since. His *Summa Theologiae* shaped Catholic doctrine on all fronts. He reflected on homosexuality in a particularly homophobic period of history, and also a time when the church began to enforce conformity of belief and practice, and orthodox theologians were viewed as infallible exponents of Christian doctrine. "In the end Aquinas admits more or less frankly that his categorization of homosexual acts as 'unnatural' is a concession to popular sentiment," Boswell concludes a lengthy examination of the theologian's work. "Aquinas could bring to bear no argument against homosexual behavior which would make it more serious than overeating and admitted, moreover, that homosexual desire was the result of a 'natural' condition, which would logically have made behavior resulting from it not only inculpable but 'good'"[4] in terms of Aquinas's own explication of natural law.

Ultimately, in appeals to nature, what was "natural" was determined by majority experience and opinion, a kind of "reason" that was nonetheless instinctual, and "a curious combination of utopian ideals and empirical observation, with little relation either to reality or Christian teaching."[5] Today's expressions of natural law decry homosexuality, while allowing lending money at interest, in the eyes of the church a far more grievous, excommunicable, and unnatural act in medieval times because the lender did nothing to earn it, and the money grew "unnaturally."[6]

Christian moral teaching is largely *counter* natural. Loving God, neighbor, and enemies is not something readily evident in the animal kingdom. Monogamy or mating for life is practiced by very few species. Mutuality in coupling or participation of both parents in child rearing is not common. Responsibility in mating is rare. Sin is unknown. Though nature may serve as a natural sacrament of the presence, wonder, and providence of God, it is not the source of Christian ethical behavior, nor necessary evidence of the sacred in marriage.

Marriage as a Sacrament

Roman Catholic tradition recognizes marriage as a sacrament, but generally Protestants, at least officially, do not. In a debate on the ordination of gay people in my own denomination, which does not recognize marriage as a sacrament, someone suggested we should first approve same-gender marriage. An audible gasp went through the room, as if marriage were more sacrosanct than ordination! Even in a tradition that does not officially view marriage as a sacrament, the *de facto* sentiment was present.

A sacrament is a ritual in which an unseen God reveals a visible and tangible presence to true believers, an outward and visible sign of an inward and spiritual grace.[7] It may serve as an "instrument of sanctification."[8] By their sensual nature, sacraments remind us that spirituality is not necessarily an out-of-body experience and that our bodies are sacred—temples in which God's Spirit is happy to dwell. The Word is made flesh once again, so to speak, not by us, but by God. At the wedding in Cana, an event in the life of Jesus which lends credence to considering marriage a sacrament, Jesus transforms ordinary water, mysteriously and mystically but no less materially, into wine—symbolic, I believe, of the holy transformation of matrimony. The ordinary becomes extraordinary in what Thomas Moore calls "the alchemy of marriage."[9] Studies verify the miracle, revealing that married people live happier, healthier, and longer lives than single people and even couples who simply live together.[10] Through the agency of the divine, in this case, embodied in Jesus, a better wine is produced than we can produce ourselves, evidenced by the wine steward who commends the bridegroom for saving the best wine for last (John 2:10). That's what happens in *true lovemaking*, that is, *the making of love through caring and commitment as well as touch*. Ordinary sensations manifest divine realities, another Celtic "thin place" where heaven and earth touch. Children often mock older brothers and sisters when they kiss or have crushes or enjoy holding hands, because the younger siblings have not yet experienced the transformation that comes in these limited experiences of lovemaking. The sacramental qualities of lovemaking require participation to fully understand. There is a parallel: early Christians did not explain to converts the meaning of the sacraments of baptism and the Eucharist until after their first partaking because it was believed that one could only understand a sacrament after receiving its blessing. And just as we offer a prayer of thanksgiving after receiving the Eucharist, so our sighs in lovemaking may unconsciously give voice to our wonder and praise of God.

Often denied the sacraments, I believe that many faithful gay men and lesbians came to understand our lovemaking (the making of love through caring and commitment as well as touch) as a means of transcendent grace, an experience of the holy, a recognition of the image of God in the other as well as in ourselves, a manifestation of heaven on earth, God's holy gift to us. This is not to say that gay people, like straight people, did not trample on the holy, or participate in sexual encounters without discerning their sacred possibility. Nor does it mean we were always looking for God in such encounters; rather, as with all sacraments, God *was looking for us*. As a lesbian with no religious background explained her reason for attending a workshop I led on the church and homosexuality: "In making love with my lover, I got in touch with a spiritual realm I never before experienced. Since spirituality has to do with God, I came here to find out about God."

My first stirrings as a young boy were not explicitly sexual—they were to be with someone of my own gender for a lifetime, something I hardly thought possible. My first gay experience occurred in late high school and early college, when I fell in love with my best male friend. It was not and never became a sexual encounter. It was an emotional, soulful passion. It was neither something I sought, nor learned, nor chose. Like so many things of God, it chose me. I loved this man "as my own soul," as Jonathan loved David. I chose chastity—the subordination of desire to responsibility—refusing to exploit the friendship by sexually fantasizing about him. Yet the feelings I had for him served as my first inkling that my sexuality was given to me for good, not for evil, to paraphrase Joseph's reconciling words to his brothers about the evil way they outcast him from the family. I believed at the time and believe still that all ability to love is ultimately a gift from God; thus I had to accept God's gift of my ability to love someone of my own gender. My years of pastoral experience within the lesbian and gay and bisexual and transgender community have confirmed that mine was not an uncommon experience.

Since seminary, I have officiated at dozens of marriage ceremonies, for gay couples and for straight couples. Through premarital counseling, I discouraged those who were looking to marriage as a magical "fix" for ills in their relationship or in their individual lives. I carefully explained that the ceremony would be simply one more step on the path of their relationship. Every ceremony I performed gave me a great deal of joy. But I never understood how transforming marriage could be until my partner urged me to have a ceremony with him. One hundred people crowded into our small neighborhood church in Atlanta for our "Ceremony of the Heart," celebrated by our pastor. We were exuberant as we confessed our love and covenant in the presence of family, friends, and our congregation, seeking their blessing and support. As we faced each other, exchanging vows, I was overwhelmed by the sacred nature of our commitment and the sacred nature of the man who stood before me. I became a different person, a better person. It was a kind of conversion experience—like being born again. I didn't even think "civil right." Rather, it felt like a holy responsibility, a sacred calling. Until I had such firsthand experience, I would never have known how transfiguring marriage could be. It was much more than "another step" in our relationship. We glowed like Moses coming down the mountaintop as we walked down the aisle after having had our covenant blessed.

At that moment, I would have taken issue with Martin Luther's view that marriage conferred "no sanctifying grace" as a sacrament should.[11] Rather, I would have affirmed the Roman Catholic view that marriage transformed me as baptism had and that it transformed our relationship.[12] I would, however, have disagreed that it was our mere exchange of vows that made our marriage sacramental, the basis of early canon law.[13] At heart I was too Calvinist for that, because I believed the moment was made holy not only by our exchange of vows and rings, but also by the affirmation of family, friends, and spiritual community surrounding us, the blessing and confirmation of the two ministers officiating, the holy liturgy of scriptures, sermon, prayers, ritual, hymns and sacred music, all in the sanctuary hallowed by our home congregation. The only thing missing was legal validation.

In John Calvin's more developed theology of marriage as a covenant among many, not just between the couple, "This involvement of parents, peers, ministers, and magistrates in the formation of marriage was not an idle or dispensable ceremony. These four parties represented different dimensions of God's involvement in the marriage covenant, and they were thus essential to the legitimacy of the marriage itself. To omit any such party in the formation of the marriage was, in effect, to omit God from the marriage covenant."[14] Because of our value separating church and state, most Americans no longer view government validation (magistrates) as representative of God's participation. Yet most Americans still do not fully recognize a marriage without government validation.

Sacraments Require Believers

Sacraments require the participation of believers. Those gathered that day for our ceremony apparently believed, or at least practiced the will to believe. Believers each have a different experience of a sacramental event, both in level of intensity and in individual meaning, but they unite in their opinion that God is somehow manifestly present. Baptists and Catholics, for example, have a very different way of understanding the central Christian sacrament, even using different terms, Communion and Eucharist. They may not concelebrate, but at least in modern times, they don't go after each other for celebrating the sacrament differently and bringing different meanings to Christ's table.

In the ecumenical divinity school I attended, the Baptists once leading us in Communion substituted trays of grape juice in individual tiny glasses for our usual chalices of wine. One of the celebrants accidentally dropped the consecrated loaf, scattering bread crumbs all over the floor, picking it up and probably not giving it another thought, other than possibly the five-second rule about food dropped on the floor. But those from other liturgical traditions were on the floor after the service carefully picking up all the holy crumbs. Yet I would think true believers would consider that observance of the sacrament no less real and God no less present than in a more formal celebration.

Yet when it comes to the genders involved, marriage is a sacrament or near-sacrament that cannot similarly be "stretched" in some people's minds, which implies its holiness is greater than that of the Eucharist! When it comes to joining those of the same gender, marriage is "untouchable" and inflexible as Mt. Sinai. But when it comes to joining those of the opposite gender, marriage is quite accessible and malleable, as explained in the previous chapter. As difficult as an ecumenical observance of Holy Communion may be, the challenge pales in comparison to an observance of Holy Matrimony between same-gender partners for most Christians. As with any sacrament, "eyes of faith" are required. In the Eucharist, those who do not share our Christian faith will only see us consume bread and wine and may not recognize the body and blood of Christ or the participation in the life, death, and resurrection of Christ that it signifies. In similar fashion, those who do not believe in same-gender marriage may only see the sexual nature of the relationship, or its surface aspects, such as gender, not looking deeply enough to see an outward and visible sign of inward and spiritual grace. Same-gender marriage challenges heterosexuals to equate homosexual partnering and their own, something that they may never have had to do before. On the other hand, gay people out of necessity are quite adept at equating heterosexual pairing and our own, as we have had to translate into our own experience almost every romance or marriage we've witnessed in real life as well as through the arts and the media. In other words, we have more experience with opposite-gender marriage than straight people have with same-gender marriage. As one elderly woman said to me upon seeing two men hug: "It's just that we're not used to it yet."

To paraphrase comedienne Robin Tyler, "When a straight couple reveal their relationship, it's called *sharing*. When a gay couple reveals their relationship, it's called *flaunting*." When our ceremony was announced in the *Atlanta Journal-Constitution*, just like opposite-gender weddings, "nonbelievers" in our marriage challenged our pastor, the Rev. Peter Denlea, in a presbytery meeting, wanting him reprimanded and our blessing undone. Our pastor gave an impassioned speech about his own transformation as an Irish Catholic career Navy bomber pilot from Boston's tough Southie neighborhood who thought he knew what homosexuals were until, in retirement, he became a Presbyterian pastor serving a neighborhood which included lesbian and gay couples and singles. All the delegates to the meeting may not have agreed with him, but they gave him a prolonged ovation after his impassioned speech and took no action against him or the blessing.

Another pastor commented that undoing our blessing would be like undoing the ringing of a bell. In the first chapter of this book, I described Jacob wrestling with God. Earlier he had stolen his father's blessing from Esau. Though it was stolen, the blessing was his. No one disputed this. Even if those who opposed our marriage viewed us as somehow stealing their blessing, it was impossible to "unbless" us, just as the same-gender marriages performed to date cannot be undone by outside forces, spiritually speaking. "What God has joined together, let no one separate."

In Spirit and In Truth

Jews of Jesus' day viewed Samaritans with disgust because they were of mixed race, half Jew and half Arab, and worshiped in the wrong way and the wrong place. Even today, Samaritans are not held in high regard. Yet, to demonstrate what to do to inherit eternal life, Jesus held up as a model a "good" Samaritan, which biblical scholar James Sanders has said would be like holding up as a model to present-day Christians a homosexual communist! For the first woman evangelist, Jesus picked a Samaritan woman with a questionable sexual history and doubtful relationship. To her he revealed his true identity as Messiah after saying it didn't matter where or how one worshiped (form) but "true worshipers will worship . . . in spirit and in truth" (content). In both stories, content is given priority over form.

That's because there's something magnanimous about Jesus, loving neighbors, outcasts, strangers, and enemies, and something magnanimous about the God he proclaimed, who blesses the righteous and unrighteous equally with sun and rain. They both look on the heart rather than the surface or category, just as God looked on the heart in choosing David as king (1 Samuel 16:1–13, especially verse 7). Our faith manifests wholeness; thus Jesus says in several instances, "Your faith has made you whole." Our motives are important. Our way of thinking, our attitude, our approach is spiritually vital. Why else would Jesus say that adultery begins with the lust of the heart, regardless of whether the act is committed? The Holy Spirit also proved magnanimous, as demonstrated in the Acts of the Apostles, empowering the disciples to proclaim the gospel in the languages of strangers at Pentecost (breaking down cultural boundaries), to pronounce all foods clean (the end of purity laws), and circumcision a matter of indifference (the end of discrimination against Gentiles). This seemingly nondiscriminating Spirit even poured itself out onto unclean, uncircumcised, unbaptized Gentiles. "I truly understand that God shows no partiality," Peter declared of the unclean Cornelius in Acts 10:34, no longer defining Christianity by whom it excludes, but by what it expects: "But in every nation anyone who fears [God] and does what is right is acceptable to [God]." In *Gay Marriage*, Rauch argues the same about marriage, that marriage would best be defined not by whom it excludes but by what it expects.[15]

This magnanimous approach was countercultural in Jesus' time. "Ancient cultures generally assumed a world of 'limited good,' not the expanding universe of modern capitalism," L. William Countryman writes, thus "they tended to define the fundamental offense against property as greed rather than, say, theft. Acquisition of new wealth could fall under this condemnation even when fully legal, if it were seen as gained at the expense of another."[16] Yet Jesus contrarily said if someone asked for your coat, give your cloak as well; if a Roman soldier compelled you to carry his gear one mile, the legal limit, carry it twice as far.

At least some of the loudest opponents to same-gender marriage appear to be coming from a similar "world of limited good," as if there are only so many marriage licenses—if we give them to lesbians and gay men there won't be enough for us. Or, though we've defined marriage in so many ways ourselves, if we "redefine" it to include same gender couples, the term will lose its potency. Or, the institution of marriage is "set apart" for a man and a woman, defined by whom it excludes, and for the institution to become inclusive to same-gender couples who affirm its value is to diminish rather than expand its sacred worth. It's hard for some to hear that there is enough marriage for everyone, and that the institution will be strengthened rather than diminished by becoming inclusive of same-gender couples. Treating marriage as a private club instead of a public sacred trust is the problem.

The gospel that Jesus proclaimed and that the early church interpreted, inspired by the Holy Spirit, is of an inbreaking kingdom or spiritual commonwealth of God that overcomes a world of limited resources. Baptismal water is bountiful enough to baptize unclean Gentiles (*and* Ethiopian eunuchs) who have already been baptized with the Holy Spirit—there are plenty of baptismal certificates to go around, so to speak. Multiple and diverse religious traditions and denominations have laid claim to the name "Christian" and yet the term retains its potency. The institution of the church, the *ecclesia* or "called out" ones, is at its sacred best when it is evangelical and thus inclusive of the broadest spectrum of people who confess Christ as Lord. Christians grew as a movement as they realized there was enough water and Spirit to baptize the world, that being Christian called us to ecumenism and connectionalism among very different kinds of Christians, and to follow Christ required breaking out of human boundaries and customs to be inclusive. When the church or a particular congregation treats itself as a private club is when it is least effective in its Christian mission.

Short of the Passion itself, the most impressive illustrations of this expansive way of viewing the universe and overcoming a theology of scarcity are the stories of Jesus feeding multitudes with a few loaves and fishes. His disciples feared there would not be enough to go around, but Jesus knew that even limited resources, blessed by God through prayer *and shared*, multiply. So, I believe, it is with marriage. It's a gift that keeps on giving, expansive in its ability to bless couples, no matter their gender.

Sacred Purpose of Marriage

The most ancient of the two creation stories in Genesis, found in its second chapter, reveals that God's purpose in "marriage" was that the first human creature not be alone. I place the term marriage in quotation marks because, as an institution or a word, it had not been socially constructed, though one could argue from the text, as Jesus did, that God intended the first couple to be one flesh. It was the first arranged marriage, and it was of two who were related, because Eve was taken from Adam's side, giving new meaning to "next of kin." They were vegetarians, given the task of tilling and caretaking the garden. They were naked and not ashamed, indicating that shame about our bodies and our sexuality came into the world not through God's initiative but through our own, as a result of succumbing to the temptation to be as God, an ongoing and pervasive human predilection. To those who have argued (strangely) that homosexuality is somehow a result of the Fall, the first human sin that caused expulsion from the garden, I like to point out that Adam and Eve did not sexually "know" one another until after the Fall, thus *heterosexual* expression is more directly the result! On a bad day with the kids, parents might even add *procreation* as some kind of divine retribution! Certainly, in the story, the pain of childbirth is the woman's punishment for disobedience, while that of the man is to be a breadwinner by the sweat of his brow. From this story, Protestantism has emphasized companionship as the sacred purpose of marriage.

The chronologically later creation story found in the first chapter of Genesis depicts God repeatedly declaring everything created "good," which is an important basis on which to assert that created diversity is good and that all of creation is sacred. Finally God created humankind in the image of God, male and female, and God blessed them and told them to "be fruitful and multiply." They were to have dominion over creation in the sense of being God's representatives and thus stewards of all living things, and all animals, including the human beings, were given plants to eat. From this story, Roman Catholicism has emphasized procreation as the sacred purpose of marriage.

Both Christian traditions acknowledge the importance of both marital purposes; it's a matter of emphasis, though Catholic tradition only in recent decades set aside canon law that, on paper at least, invalidated a marriage in which one party was sterile. Interestingly, neither tradition calls us to be vegetarian, nor do the most literalist of readers of the Bible, some of whom nonetheless read into the stories' silence on homosexuality a prohibition. I like to point out that the Garden of Eden story is also silent on urban dwellers and factory workers, but they are no less created in the image of God!

Countryman provides helpful observations of Jesus' treatment of these creation stories in the text regarding divorce discussed earlier in Chapter Two, Matthew 19:3–12. In response to a question about the law permitting men to divorce wives, Jesus appeals to both creation stories in significant ways. Countryman explains:

> Jesus, relying on the first creation account in Genesis (1:27), argued that the female was as human as the male: "from the beginning He made them male and female." Male and female, therefore, participate equally in the image of God. Again, relying on the second creation narrative (Genesis 2:24), he held that the man and woman (or husband and wife) become "one flesh" in marriage.[17]

In effect, the allowance for men—because of their "hardness of heart"—to divorce their wives abrogated God's concept of one flesh, and the inequity of men being allowed to do so but not women conflicted with God's creation of male and female as equals made in the image of God. Jesus then proceeds to redefine adultery as divorce and remarriage, in effect, giving the woman equal sexual property rights over the man.[18]

In defense of marriage Jesus outlaws divorce, appealing, in a sense, to a higher law, that of God making a couple one flesh. I note an interesting parallel with many of the civil servants and church ministers who have themselves appealed to a higher law in state and church settings related to same-gender marriage: in the case of civil servants, the higher law is the equality of all citizens that renders anti-gay marriage laws contrary to state and federal constitutions; and, in the case of ministers, the higher law of God's equitable justice and abundant mercy that requires, as Pope John Paul II declared, "a preferential option for the poor"—in this instance, those who have few rights and no marital rights at all.

In "defense of marriage," the legislature of the state of Georgia, where I have lived for sixteen years, passed an amendment to the state constitution for voter approval in 2004 that forbids the recognition of same-gender marriages. A suggestion to outlaw divorce as well was not seriously considered. What's wrong with this picture? Jesus put it bluntly: "You hypocrite, first take the log out of your own eye" (Matthew 7:5).

Scapegoating Same-Gender Marriage

This brings me to perhaps our greatest spiritual danger, that of scapegoating. When things go wrong, we look for someone to blame— someone *other* than ourselves, of course—especially when things are already tough. I see this in myself. If I'm tired and crabby and feeling badly about myself, I am far less tolerant of others, less open to change, less welcoming of ideas, far more cynical, more likely to find fault and apply blame, looking for external reasons for my anguish. In *People of the Lie: The Hope for Healing Human Evil*, M. Scott Peck defines evil, in part, as the "unquestioned self," the individual or institution unable or unwilling to look at himself, herself, or itself critically, *especially pronounced when perceived as being threatened.*[19] He recounts his experience of such corporate evil when he was one of the Army psychiatrists assigned to evaluate what went wrong at My Lai during the Vietnam War, where American troops massacred innocent villagers. His commission found the U.S. government *collectively* to blame, beginning at the top: a presidential administration with an unquestioned policy of communist containment based on a bankrupt domino theory. Needless to say, the report got buried.

It's easier to look critically at another culture. Nazi Germany is a prime example, both of the unquestioned self and the scapegoat mechanism. Still smarting from its defeat and resulting losses of World War I and a suffering economy, Adolf Hitler and the Nazis compiled a list of scapegoat populations to blame. Jews were the largest category, but gays were also on the list and among those sent to concentration camps and murdered by the German state, and, deplorably, the only category which was not liberated by the Allies who moved homosexuals from concentration camps to regular prisons. At the beginning of one of his lectures for the Lazarus Project, John Boswell told the story of a British gentleman and a German Nazi forced to share overnight accommodations. The German was railing about Jews, how all the world's problems were caused by them. The British gentleman egged him on until, at the end of the "dialogue," the Britisher concluded, "Yes, all the world's problems are caused by Jews and bicycle riders!" The German looked astonished. "Why bicycle riders?" he asked, incredulous. The British gentleman parried, "Why Jews?"

Boswell's life's work was studying the treatment of minorities by majority cultures. During a lecture at the University of California, Los Angeles, he began by saying he would be describing a dominant culture's attitudes, fears, and myths about a minority in medieval Europe and the task of the audience was to decide whether he was depicting Jews or gay people. As an example, the one myth I remember most clearly was that of snatching Christian children. Boswell revealed at the end of his talk that the whole time he had been describing the attitude toward *both* groups! Indeed, what he discovered in his research as a medievalist was that the lot of Jews, women, and gay people in European culture paralleled one another: when one group was more tolerated, the other groups were too; but when one group fell into disfavor, all shared a similar fate. A part of his work was trying to understand the economic, historical, social, religious, and cultural factors that prompted the scapegoating of these groups. Of special concern to him was the rise of a virulent anti-gay agenda toward the conclusion of the Middle Ages, referenced in our earlier discussion of Thomas Aquinas. In *Same-Sex Unions*, Boswell admitted he was unsatisfied with his own explanation for this rise of homophobia in his earlier tome, *Christianity,*

Social Tolerance, and Homosexuality. Other scholars have confessed they also cannot adequately explain it.

What does scapegoating have to do with the sacredness of marriage? We get the term "scapegoat" based on a King James Version mistranslation of a word in Leviticus 16 that describes the practice of the ancient Hebrews sacrificing two goats during the annual Day of Atonement (Yom Kippur). Before their sacrifice, the priests projected the sins of the people onto the animals. One was killed outright for the priests' sins and the other, for the people's sins, died by excommunication, sent off into the wilderness to die, bereft of the community's shelter, food, and water. The animals were not killed or excommunicated to placate an angry God, but rather to purify the people so they may continue to enjoy God's holy presence, as their sins died or were exiled with the animals. In a previous work, *Coming Out as Sacrament*, I've described how lesbians, gay men, and bisexual and transgender persons have suffered similar sacrifice and excommunication to preserve the peace, unity, and purity of the church—in other words, its holiness, wholeness, and distinctness.[20]

I would observe that resistance to same-gender marriage is acting out of the same principle. In this view, to keep marriage holy, to ensure God's blessing, same-gender couples must be sacrificed and excommunicated from the marital estate. Otherwise marriage itself will be tainted with impurity, as challenged in Chapter Two, and "traditional" family values assailed, as challenged in Chapter Three. Yet the sins of divorce, adultery, abandonment, incest, and abuse that haunt marriage and family these days cannot really be projected onto gay and lesbian couples, and these acts are what defile, befoul, and profane the sacred nature of marriage, not additional couples willing to embrace its spiritual discipline. Heterosexuals must confess their own sins, not project them onto homosexuals. We have our own sins to confess, though homosexuality is not one of them.

Marriage and family have had rough times of late which can basically be summed up in a catch phrase of a recent presidential campaign, "It's the economy, stupid!" In an article for *Open Hands* magazine entitled "Sexual Ethics in an Overpopulated World: Pollution, Purity, Property, and Procreation," Christian social ethicist Carol Robb describes how scapegoating obscures market and economic factors that have contributed to the destabilization of the family:

> I believe the contemporary conservative obsession with matters
> pertaining to abortion and sexuality is a substitute for our deep
> concern about economic security. Ethicist Gerard Fourez finds
> an analogue in the nineteenth century's Victorian focus on sex-
> ual ethics, while industrialization was depriving people of basic
> economic security. At a time such as this, an obsession with sex
> diverts attention to peripheral elements rather than the central
> one of a society's structures and practices, making it possible to
> conceal problems these structures and practices have created.[21]

This is an example of "the unquestioned self," in this case, a society not willing to look at itself critically to determine the actual factors troubling its people. Robb explains how today globalization and economic dislocation separate marriage partners and family members, and yet, mentioning a then current controversy, the U.S. Surgeon General was fired for suggesting masturbation should be discussed in sex education programs, diverting the attention of many churchgoers from the larger economic issues that are subverting the family.

More than one political observer noted that the Georgia legislators to whom I earlier alluded spent so much time on the antigay marriage amendment, they couldn't address the issues that are truly plaguing the state, including ranking fiftieth in education! They had to return for a special session at enormous taxpayer expense to finish their other business. When we can't look critically at ourselves and solve the real problems with which marriages and families contend, it is so easy to point the finger at those who haven't even had a chance to fail at marriage.

Traditional Same-Sex Unions: A Love without Pretense

Yale scholar John Boswell's unearthing of liturgies for same-gender couples up through the Middle Ages and even beyond reads like a mystery novel. After his book *Christianity, Social Tolerance, and Homosexuality* appeared in 1980, he received an "anonymous tip" to look at a certain page in an early book of liturgies. There he found a same-gender ceremony. He began researching every extant copy of the liturgy, spending summers in public and monastic libraries throughout Europe, including the Vatican, and his exacting scholarship delayed his publishing the book on *Same-Sex Unions* until 1994, shortly before his untimely death.

In the meanwhile, two friends of mine, also scholars, invited me to preside at their own Rite of Spiritual Brotherhood based on this ancient ceremony. A centerpiece of the liturgy is the invoking of the names, love, and martyrdom of two male saints, Serge and Bacchus, who share the same feast day of October 7. (Interestingly, Metropolitan Community Churches, an international denomination which largely embraces LGBT people and their families and friends, was founded on October 6, 1968.)

Serge and Bacchus were soldiers in the Roman army in the late third and early fourth century. Favorites of Emperor Maximian, they fell into disfavor when they refused to worship the emperor's idols (one of the reasons early Christians did not serve in the military, as emperor worship was required of Roman soldiers) and confessed their Christian faith. According to Boswell, the texts describing their relationship use a word which translates "lovers." This seems confirmed by their initial punishment, being ridiculed while paraded through city streets in women's clothing. As a sign of unity, they sang together Psalm 23, changing the "I" wording to "we." Tortured, Bacchus died, but appeared to Serge in a vision in prison. Radiant, Bacchus told Serge they were "bound together" forever and would be reunited, and that "your crown of justice is me, my crown of justice is you." (Crowning was a part of opposite-gender ceremonies of the time.) After additional torture, Serge was beheaded. One chronicler described them in this way: "They were as one in the love of Jesus Christ and inseparable as spiritual brothers. They were like stars shining joyously over the earth, radiating the light of profession of and faith in our savior and Lord Jesus Christ."[22]

The rite that Boswell found in a number of sources included the Lord's Prayer, a sung Gloria, Prayers of the Faithful, scriptures, hymns, a homily (in which Serge and Bacchus might be lifted up), prayers (one offered by the celebrant, the second by the congregation), the couple's joint recitation of Psalm 23 in first person plural form, followed by the couple kissing the Bible, and offering the Peace.

The following are the prayers as translated by one of the men who asked me to preside at their ceremony:

> Let us pray to the Lord.
> O Lord our God, you who have granted to us all things that tend toward our salvation, you who have also commanded us to love each other, and to forgive each other for our offenses, you yourself, compassionate Lord, since your servants have already been joined to one another in love, we ask you to grant them a faith unconfounded and a love without pretense. As you gave your peace to your holy disciples, so on them confer everything necessary for salvation and life eternal. This we pray through Jesus Christ, your son, our Lord, who lives and reigns with you now and forever. Amen.
>
> Let us pray to the Lord.
> Lord God Almighty, creator of heaven and earth, you who have made humanity in your image and likeness, and have willed that your holy martyrs Serge and Bacchus be joined by a bond not of nature, but of faith and the Holy Spirit, we ask that you yourself Lord, having already sent your Holy Spirit over these your servants who come before you to receive your grace, that you grant them also a faith unconfounded and a love without pretense, to converse without bitterness and offense one against the other. For yours is the kingdom, and the power, and the glory, now and forever. Amen.[23]

The contexts of this liturgy reinforce Boswell's argument that it is a form of same-gender marriage. The earliest Greek manuscript from eighth-century Italy includes four sacramental unions: heterosexual betrothal (the customary stage prior to marriage), two heterosexual marriage ceremonies, and a similar service joining two men.[24] By the twelfth century, what had initially been a simple ceremony of prayers of blessing had developed, as had its heterosexual counterpart, into a full office, which included lit candles, placing hands on the Gospel, joining of their right hands (a common Roman marriage gesture), and binding them with the celebrant's stole, an initial litany, crowning (common in heterosexual marriages, though less frequent in same-sex ceremonies), recitation of the Lord's Prayer, Communion, a kiss, occasionally circling the altar, followed by a banquet for family and friends.[25] The ceremony, according to Boswell, occurred in a variety of contexts in liturgical collections, "but by far the most common context is marriage, usually in the following order: heterosexual betrothal, ceremony for a first heterosexual marriage, ceremony for a second heterosexual marriage (a different office, with less emphasis on procreation), office of same-sex union."[26] Boswell concludes, "According to the modern conception [of marriage]—i.e., a permanent emotional union acknowledged in some way by the community—it was unequivocally a marriage."[27]

The Dominican Jacobus Goar published the ceremony in his collection of Greek liturgies most commonly referred to as *Euchologia* in Paris in 1647, conceding it as a matter of public record but as a ceremony that could no longer be performed legally, though there were no laws against it at the time. He labeled it as a rite of spiritual friendship or brotherhood, even though the word "spiritual" does not appear in the ceremony and love, not friendship or brotherhood, is celebrated in the text itself. As Boswell points out, it could not have been simply intended for friends or brotherhood or sisterhood or purely spiritual relationships, as it was expressly forbidden to monks who might be expected to have such spiritual relationships, and the rite was only celebrated for a pair, never for multiple "friends." In addition, as explained in Chapter Three, Christians already considered themselves brothers and sisters, so such a ceremony to celebrate brotherhood or sisterhood would have been redundant.

Of course there have been critics of Boswell's analysis, especially of premature reports of his research before he was satisfied enough to publish his results. As someone who knew him, I have never met nor read a more meticulous scholar or researcher. He was personally a man of enormous integrity and honesty and grace, as well as intellectual capacity. He was also a thoroughly committed and passionate Christian, intentionally joining the Roman Catholic Church as a teenager with a Presbyterian upbringing. In the final analysis, what has not been questioned, and what is the most important result of his findings for me as well as for the purpose of this book, is that the kinship of same-gender couples found blessing in the church. As Boswell himself suggests, whether or not such marriages were sexually consummated is as little known as whether childless heterosexual marriages were. Marriage goes deeper than sex, as the final chapter will discuss.

Esau was the firstborn, yet Jacob received his father's blessing and God's blessing. Same-gender couples may not have been the firstborn of Eden, so to speak, yet received the church's blessing during a period when marriage and procreation were not high priorities for the church. In our present time, when being fruitful and multiplying is not a high priority for an overpopulated world, perhaps a middle ground could be found in which both straight and gay couples may enjoy the blessings of the church.

Notes

[1] Rogers, *Reading the Bible and the Confessions*, 29.

[2] J. Philip Newell, *Listening for the Heartbeat of God: A Celtic Spirituality* (Mahwah, NJ: Paulist Press, 1997), 29.

[3] Henri J. M. Nouwen, *Creative Ministry: Beyond Professionalism in Teaching, Preaching, Counseling, Organizing, and Celebrating* (Garden City, NY: Doubleday & Company, Inc., 1971), 103.

[4] John Boswell, *Christianity, Social Tolerance, and Homosexuality: Gay People in Western Europe from the Beginning of the Christian Era to the Fourteenth Century* (Chicago: The University of Chicago Press, 1980), 328.

[5] Boswell, *Christianity, Social Tolerance, and Homosexuality*, 314.

[6] Boswell, *Christianity, Social Tolerance, and Homosexuality*, 330–332.

[7] Augustine of Hippo described a sacrament as "a visible sign of an invisible grace" and Paul VI called it "a reality imbued with the hidden presence of God."

[8] Witte, *From Sacrament to Contract*, 27.

[9] Thomas Moore, *Soul Mates: Honoring the Mysteries of Love and Relationship* (New York: HarperPerennial, 1994), Chapter 3.

[10] Rauch, *Gay Marriage*, 23.

[11] Witte, *From Sacrament to Contract*, 5, 52.

[12] Witte, 27.

[13] Witte, 28.

[14] Witte, 95–96.

[15] Rauch, *Gay Marriage*, 97.

[16] Countryman, *Dirt, Greed and Sex*, 148.

[17] Countryman, 174. See also Elisabeth Schüssler Fiorenza's *In Memory of Her: A Feminist Theological Reconstruction of Christian Origins* (New York: Crossroads, 10th edition, 1994), 143.

[18] Countryman, *Dirt, Greed and Sex*, 175.

[19] M. Scott Peck, *People of the Lie: The Hope for Healing Human Evil* (New York: Simon & Schuster, 1983), especially Chapter 6.

[20] Glaser, *Coming Out as Sacrament*, Chapter Two, "Sacrifices and Scapegoats."

[21] Carol Robb, "Sexual Ethics in an Overpopulated World: Pollution, Purity, Property, and Procreation," *Open Hands,* Vol. 13, No. 4 (Spring 1998), 11. She references Gerard Fourez, *Liberation Ethics* (Philadelphia: Temple University, 1982), 111. See also Carol Robb's *Equal Value: An Ethical Approach to Economics and Sex* (Beacon Press, 1995). The *Open Hands* article was adapted from a presentation to the Restoring Creation Conference, Ghost Ranch Conference Center, Abiquiu, New Mexico, June 24–28, 1996.

[22] *[Old] Catholic Encyclopedia*, 728, and Dr. John Boswell, Lazarus Lectures, West Hollywood Presbyterian Church.

[23] Prayers from the Greek *Euchologia*, ed. Jacobus Goar (Paris:1647), translated by Mark Infusino.

[24] Boswell, 178.

[25] Boswell, 185.

[26] Boswell, 186–187.

[27] Boswell, 190.

CHAPTER FIVE

Sex and the Body of Christ

"If one member suffers, all suffer together with it; if one member is honored, all rejoice together with it. Now you are the body of Christ and individually members of it."
— The apostle Paul in 1 Corinthians 12:26–27

A committee of the West Hollywood Presbyterian Church scheduled a Safer Sex seminar for a Sunday night. The organizers overlooked the fact that a 12-step meeting used our fellowship hall on Sunday evenings, so we were forced to hold the event in the sanctuary. I was stunned by the uneasiness apparent among the participants about talking of sexual matters in the same place they spoke, sung, and prayed about spiritual matters. Though demographics and conscious outreach have since made the congregation more diverse, most who attended at the time were gay or lesbian or bisexual—and I prejudicially thought that they would not be reticent discussing sexuality in a spiritual locale, especially given that we occasionally reflected on how our sexuality could be an expression of our spirituality in that very sanctuary.

The presenter from AIDS Project Los Angeles voiced what many were feeling. He confessed that, as the son of a Lutheran pastor, he felt awkward giving his "secular" talk on safer sex from a pulpit. As he proceeded—rather valiantly—to do so, it seemed to me that though he was a fine presenter, he offered information more hesitantly than he might have done otherwise, and people likewise phrased their questions more delicately.

In my view, this experience served as one more demonstration of how separated sexuality and spirituality are in our popular mindset. I believe that the taboo that prompts reverence in a sacred space is positive and appropriate. But to believe sexuality, a creation and a gift from God, is not holy, sets us up for a failure to recognize the sacred possibilities and responsibilities of every caress and every sexual encounter. And to think that some spaces are more holy than others on this earth sets us up for failures of recognition of our neighborhoods and environments as sacred.

As I implied in the epilogue to my first book, *Uncommon Calling*, until we can say a prayer of thanks to God for what we receive in the bedroom just as we offer thanks for what we receive in the dining room,[1] we will not fully enjoy the inbreaking, loving commonwealth of God available within our sexual encounters. And the presenter's notion that one can give a "secular" talk on sexuality, though a common opinion, belies the sacred nature of sexuality. After all, Eros was not only a god in the Greek pantheon, but in two of three traditions was considered one of the most ancient of all the gods, in one tradition designated as "the firstborn."[2] And, in relation to marriage, even the non-religious recognize its ancient sacred mystery in the so-called naturalist view described in the work of John Witte, Jr. in Chapter Three.

I confess I did not intend to write this chapter on "Sex and the Body of Christ." It grew from what I needed to say to proceed with proposing my view in the following chapter that Christian marriage—same-gender and opposite-gender—is ultimately a spiritual discipline. And, like the son of the Lutheran pastor sheepishly talking about sex from a pulpit, some of what follows made me as uncomfortable to write as it will make some readers uncomfortable to read. Integrating our spiritual and sexual selves is a lifelong process. I offer my own "work in progress" so that the reader may know I am very aware that I am only a fellow pilgrim in this endeavor to transform sex-negativity into sex-positivity, to pronounce all parts of the body "good" just as God pronounced all parts of creation "good" in Genesis 1. I believe the inbreaking commonwealth of God echoes the Paradise of Eden in which we strolled with God naked and unashamed.

What Would Jesus Do?

Through his letters to the first Christian congregations, the apostle Paul addresses particular issues that arose in the early church. One of his primary concerns was that "everyone just get along" until Christ's return. Another concern was that the spiritual community maintain its separate, holy (a word which literally means "set apart") identity from the surrounding culture, a holiness based not on law but on our belonging to Christ. "Don't judge," he tells the religious legalists at the church of Rome, and follows it with one of his strongest arguments for relying on God's grace, a reliance that would build the community summarized both transcendently ("Do not be conformed to this world . . . ," " . . . we are one body in Christ") and practically ("Live in harmony with one another," "Welcome those who are weak in faith, but not for the purpose of quarreling over opinions") in Romans chapters 12–15.

But in 1 Corinthians, he urges the church at Corinth to judge, excluding one of its members for a sexual sin:

> Indeed, a member of the church had actually married his stepmother (presumably after the death of his father) (5:1). Such an act certainly violated Jewish law (Leviticus 18:8, 20:11). It also violated Roman law. . . . However, Paul's objection to this act is not grounded in law per se. Rather, Paul's objection to all *porneia* [sexual immorality], whatever its particular form, is grounded in his concepts of the resurrection of the body, the oneness of the body with Christ, and the sanctifying of the body through the Spirit (6:13–15, 17, 19).[3]

Christians belong to Christ. We are one with him. We are his body. Therefore, do not exploit a sex worker because Christ would never do so (6:15–17).[4] Avoid sexual immorality (7:2). Do not deprive your spouse of conjugal rights (7:3). Do not divorce (7:10–11). Your body is a temple of the Holy Spirit (6:19, where the "you" is singular, meaning the individual Christian). You were bought with a price (6:20). You, the church, are also God's temple (3:16, where the "you" is plural, thus the collective community), and therefore the man who married his stepmother must be removed (5:2), essentially excommunicated. Paul clarifies that whereas the church should be exclusive of such a person, in no way can its members avoid associating with such people in every-day life "since you would then need to go out of the world" (5:10). (I highlight this last admonition because it suggests that Christians who might seek antigay civil legislation based on their sense of sexual moral-ity are out of sync with Paul's counsel. Paul's guidance on sexual matters is for the church, not the culture, and for the church to impose its own spiritual disciplines on the culture would contravene Paul's other con-cern that the church "get along" with those outside the faith, especially evidenced in Romans 13:1–7 that begins "Let every person be subject to the governing authorities. . . .")

It is in this broader context that Paul reminds the Corinthians that "wrongdoers will not inherit the kingdom of God" (see Corinthians 6:9–11). The list of wrongdoers that follows comes early in the discussion on sexual morality and may serve a somewhat similar purpose as that of the diatribe in Romans, that of setting up his "case." The list, common to moralizers of his time and not unique to Paul, includes the Greek words *malakoi,* which literally means *soft,* implying moral weakness, and *arse-nokoitai,* which literally means *males who go to bed.* Through the ages, these words have been variously translated, separately or combined, as "effeminate," "abusers of themselves with mankind," "masturbators," "homosexuals," "sexual perverts," "male prostitutes," and "sodomites." Boswell, in *Christianity, Social Tolerance, and Homosexuality,* points out that the early Church Fathers used *arsenokoitai* in heterosexual contexts, and other modern commentators have suggested the reference may be to gigolos who married rich older women to inherit their wealth. Boswell explains that the early Church Fathers, while commenting in detail on 1 Corinthians, never noted in this passage a reference to homosexuality, a subject on which they were not reticent.

In an extensive footnote in Boswell's subsequent *Same-Sex Unions in Premodern Europe,* Boswell takes on critics of his earlier interpretation, introducing his previous omission of the association of *arsenokoitai* with Sodom in the writings of Eusebius.[5] But because homosexuality was not addressed as a *condition* in ancient times as it is today, but rather as a *practice,* Boswell argues, the reference is to anal intercourse.

Bolstering this conclusion, he explains, the term *arsenokoitai* is used and the practice more explicitly described and condemned in male-female contexts, and, interestingly, given more severe penances than in male-male contexts. My own assessment of this latter peculiarity is that those in male-female intercourse were perceived as having a "natural" choice of orifice.

To be the receptor of intercourse as a male would have been to surrender one's maleness, a significant taboo in a patriarchal culture. This is confirmed by the fact that the act of the penetrator would have been more acceptable. Such intercourse was also associated with pederasty, an older male with a younger male, though, to put this in perspective, it must be noted that heterosexual couplings of the time were usually characterized by a similar age differential between an older male and a younger female.

I would imagine that some readers are squirming in their seats at the mere *thought* of anal intercourse, or at least my writing about it! Taboo is kicking in. Remember Countryman's association of taboo with bodily orifices referenced in Chapter Two. Yet it is an activity engaged in regardless of sexual orientation, both for pleasure as well as a practical means of birth control, especially for poorer or younger people without access to other means.

Custom and taboo vary widely in sexual matters. For instance, my mother, a fundamentalist Baptist in her eighties, while believing it should have remained a private matter, was nonetheless confounded by the Clinton-Lewinsky scandal. "What she did was not natural," she told me. Note the blame placed on the *woman*! Armed with a recent media report of a study of sexual practices in the United States, I explained that the vast majority of Americans engaged in oral intercourse. "Well, they didn't used to!" she exclaimed. (Let me add that both my mother and father were completely supportive and loving of me, despite their conservative religious beliefs.)

This is when our *erotophobia* surfaces, how Episcopal priest and seminary professor Carter Heyward terms our sex-negativity, discussed in Chapter Two. I have experienced it in merely writing the last several paragraphs, especially thinking of a kindly old grandmother reading them. This image alone, my fear of offending "a kindly old grandmother," is worthy of a closer look. Why did I not choose "*grandfather*"? Probably some expression of sexism, but also a belief that men, while reticent about sexual matters, have considered such things, just because men seem to think a lot about sex. My ageism is clearly at play, too, as older generations may have experienced a variety of sexual expressions. But the most interesting adjective is "kindly," as if human sexuality is not a "kindly" thing, clearly a product of my own sex-negativity. It may also be because anal intercourse is not generally perceived as a kindly or loving act, which it certainly can be. During the early days of the AIDS crisis, I heard a television news reporter declare that HIV was more likely transmitted among gay men because of the "violent" nature of their sexual act. It reveals much about a society that finds it more acceptable talking about violence rather than the particulars of anal intercourse, and that anal intercourse would necessarily be understood as violent. Sex educators would tell you that it is no more "violent" than vaginal intercourse, and both forms of intercourse may become violent in cases of force and rape.

Yet overall, my discomfort may grow from the sense that, just as my late mother thought the aforementioned sexual activity should have remained private, I believe that sexually intimate acts are best left to the partners in question and fall into the sphere of "too much information." This is not to say that the couple should not be held accountable to the community: adultery, sexually transmitted diseases, and procreation all may require resources of the community, for example. As fond as I am of psychologist Carl Rogers's adage that "what is personal is most universal," I also believe that what is private should not necessarily be universalized, i.e., held up as "the way things should be." Thus what heterosexuals do in private should not be forced on homosexuals, and vice versa.

Few of us feel comfortable imagining ourselves as the Body of Christ performing *any* sexual act, so averse are we to thinking of Jesus as a sexual actor. Think of the controversy over the film *The Last Temptation of Christ* for its suggestion that the last temptation for Jesus was that of living a normal married life. But we *are* able to imagine Jesus celebrating our sexual relationships that are loving and just, faithful to God and to one another, blessing the community and being blessed by the community.

Jesus confronted the purity emphasis of his religion. Purity regulated social boundaries and body boundaries, who could dine with whom (Jesus eating with sinners in Matthew 9:10–13), who could touch whom (holiness prevented contact with women or the sick and the dead, a concept Jesus resisted numerous times, as described in a previous chapter), and the required ritual baptizing of hands before eating (Mark 7:1–23). In the context of the latter case, Jesus accused the religious leaders of his day of holding to human tradition rather than listening for God (7:8) and then essentially declares, as earlier referenced, that it is not what goes into the body that defiles, but what comes out of a person's heart that is spiritually vital. Translating Jesus' principle to sexuality: it's not how human boundaries touch and interface, but how human virtues emerge in such relationships that has spiritual merit.

Given Paul's predilection for the freedom we enjoy in Christ, it is natural that, within the confines of his given experience, he gave latitude for people to choose their own faithful response to their sexuality: remain single, marry rather than "burn," and, if married, refrain from sexual intercourse for a season, but not permanently. He and other biblical writers judged sexual acts without having our contemporary concepts of the reproductive system, of the equality of women and men, of the spectrums of both sexual orientation and gender identity. We, as the Body of Christ in the twenty-first century, cannot pretend not to have this knowledge, and through the Holy Spirit we are given, not just permission, but the authority and the obligation to be led into further truth, to "bind and unbind" people's consciences in fresh ways. Earlier cited was the Presbyterian report that held up "justice-love" rather than heterosexual marriage as the contemporary Christian paradigm for relationships. This is a fresh way to interpret Christ's message for relationships, given our new awareness that the designation "marriage" alone does not guard against subordination, inequality, exploitation, and abuse.

The apostle Paul gives a biblical base on which to stand up for those among us with a homosexual or bisexual orientation: "Let each of you remain in the condition in which you were called" (1 Corinthians 7:24). We may not agree with all of Paul's applications of this principle—just as we no longer live by all the applications of the Holiness Code of

Leviticus, while valuing its principles of wholeness and distinctness, personal integrity and social harmony. But the principle of remaining "in the condition in which you were called" may be applied to sexual orientation. Perhaps we may also apply another principle of Paul's to same-gender marriages, one that comes three chapters later in his letter to Corinth, in the context of yet one more highly charged controversy in the early church: eating meat from animals that have been sacrificed to idols. Paul declares, "If I partake with thankfulness, why should I be denounced because of that for which I give thanks?" (10:30).

Images of Christ

As mentioned, our erotophobia may prevent us from seeing Christ sexually relating to anyone. Besides our sex-negativity, we are also restrained by the positive taboo of the holy. Just as the Hebrews were not to touch the holy mountain of Sinai or later, the Ark of the Covenant, we may be hesitant to touch the holy image of Christ. "Jesus Christ— the same yesterday, today, and forever," Hebrews 13:8 asserts. And yet the following verse, while warning of "strange teachings," affirms, "it is well for the heart to be strengthened by grace, not by regulations . . . which have not benefited those who observe them" (13:9). Remember Countryman's explanation cited in an earlier chapter that "the emphasis found in the Gospels [is] that laws exist to enhance a faithful human life, not place burdens on it."[6] Indeed, Hebrews was written, in part, to prevent early Christians from returning to old religious concepts and practices.

Seeming to contradict the taboo of touching the sacred image of Christ, another taboo calls us to be iconoclastic. We need to examine our images of Christ, reminding ourselves of the second commandment against "graven images," the holy taboo of claiming certain knowledge of God, rendered in stone, whether Moses desiring God's name at the burning bush or Mary Magdalene trying to hold onto the risen Christ at the empty tomb.

We carry a variety of images of Christ within us, many provided by Hollywood: Jeff Chandler as a stoic blue-eyed Christ in *King of Kings*, Max Von Sydow as the gaunt, apparitional Christ of *The Greatest Story*

Ever Told, the cool "celebrity" Christ of *Jesus Christ Superstar*, the hippie-like and sensual Christ of *The Last Temptation of Christ*, the bloody Christ of Mel Gibson's *The Passion of The Christ*. Perhaps the best "Hollywood" Christ is that of *Ben Hur*, in which we see Christ only in the effect he has on others, which is the witness we have, in a sense, throughout the New Testament and church tradition and the present global church.

In *Meeting Jesus Again for the First Time*, Lutheran professor Marcus Borg describes meeting a series of Christs during different periods of his life: childhood, adolescence, college, seminary, and middle age.[7] Borg's writing resonates with his readers because many of us have also had different experiences of Jesus Christ at various periods of our own lives. Each encounter with Christ may come from those teaching or guiding us at the time, our own level of maturity, personal or world events, as well as our own spiritual development. Each circumstance and combinations of these may transform our perceptions of Jesus, just, as we earlier discussed, interpretations of a given scripture may change, given circumstances—that's what makes the Bible a classic, similar to what we consider literary classics. That Christ may be experienced in different ways at different times strengthens his universal hold on us and our spiritual imagination. The reader will notice the similarity to the diverse ways in which marriage has been experienced at different times in different cultures, indicating its own universal hold on us. Rather than fear the "subjective" nature of our own experiences of Christ, it helps to remember that the biblical writers' experience of Jesus was also subjective, because they were seeing him through eyes of faith—and we wouldn't want it any other way.

An earlier book of mine, *Come Home! Reclaiming Spirituality and Community as Gay Men and Lesbians*, included a chapter on "Accepting Jesus Christ,"[8] in which I presented the four Christs traditionally available to us, an analysis neither original nor unique to me. The first is the historical Jesus of Nazareth, the primary source of which is scripture. Historians of the time rarely felt compelled to be objective and biblical writers, as just described, wrote out of their faith experience. Even as the early Christians believed that the meaning of a sacrament could not be understood before a believer took part in it, so the meaning of Jesus

Christ could not be known through "objective" accounts of those who were not part of the Christian community.

The second is the mystical Christ who interrupts us in our certainties, as he did with the zealot Saul on his road to Damascus—the One "who comes to us as One unknown" as Albert Schweitzer concluded his *Quest for the Historical Jesus*. The third is the church as the Body of Christ, through the Holy Spirit and with the mind of Christ able to be led into "further truth" and able to do "greater things." The fourth is Christ the Stranger, the "least of these" of Matthew 25, who is homeless, hungry, sick, imprisoned, naked, and a stranger in need of our ministry. In my view, "accepting Jesus Christ" meant welcoming and sometimes struggling with all of these faces of Christ.

Throughout this book, and again in this chapter, the historical Jesus' lifestyle is revealed as open and welcoming of those the religious establishment rejected. The conversation regarding homosexuality and same-gender marriage is depicted as yet another instance when Christ's Spirit has interrupted our certainties about "the way things should be." LGBT Christians are undoubtedly a part of the Body of Christ the church, as are the many who support them. And yet they are also the Stranger, the one whose rights to church membership and ministry and marriage have too long been denied.

A Loving Christ

For several years I spoke and led discussions for an interfaith spiritual community in Atlanta. One Sunday I was speaking about Thich Nhat Hanh's book *Jesus and Buddha as Brothers*, drawing parallels and explaining differences between the two founders of world religions. I explained the concept in radical Zen Buddhism of "killing the Buddha." What is meant is the need to let go of previous images and understandings of the Buddha in order to embrace a fresh experience of what it means to be the Buddha. Because I was comparing Buddha and Christ, one of the more forthright members of Midtown Spiritual Community interrupted me with a profound question, "Are you saying then that we also need to kill Christ?" She had caught the logic of Zen Buddhism and applied it to her own Christian faith. Uncomfortable by the implication of "killing" Christ, I nonetheless admitted that, though I wouldn't want to be quoted on it, there is a parallel. Just as Buddhists progress toward Enlightenment as they let go of their earlier images of Buddha, so we must be prepared to let go of our earlier images of Christ as we progress in our Christian spirituality, what could be called sanctification. Henri Nouwen used to say of Jesus' departure from the disciples that he needed to get *out of the way* so that he could *be* The Way.

Among those images that we might reconsider is that of a sexless Christ. If Jesus did not have the urges that we have sexually, he would not have been "tempted in every way as we are," as Hebrews asserts. The Bible depicts a Jesus who is not afraid to be found in compromising positions with women or men, from the several women who sensually anointed him in a variety of fashions to "the man Jesus loved" who appears in the Gospel of John with his head on Jesus' bosom during the Last Supper. This Beloved Disciple, traditionally associated with John because he only appears in his Gospel with several mentions, served as the patron saint of Celtic Christianity because his proximity to Jesus symbolized the mystic desire for intimacy with Christ and with God, leaning on his bosom, "listening for the heartbeat of God."

The popular book *The Da Vinci Code* is based on the premise of a "dark" historical rumor of the church that Jesus married Mary Magdalene and fathered children, a clearly heterosexual reading of Jesus' life. Used as evidence is Leonardo da Vinci's fresco of *The Last Supper* in which an effeminate figure sits at Jesus' right hand at table. That heterosexuals would "see" Mary Magdalene as that effeminate figure belies that da Vinci himself was homosexual and that the effeminate figure more likely represents the artist's rendering of a homosexual male, something readily "seen" by homosexual viewers of the painting.

Historically, many homosexual Christians have also read into Jesus' intimate relationship with "the Beloved Disciple" of the Gospel of John feelings parallel to theirs, if chaste, from the twelfth century saint Aelred of Rivaulx's treatise on spiritual friendship, *Mirror of Love*, to the twenty-first century Theodore Jennings book *The Man Jesus Loved*. Aelred wrote about the relationship of male monastics to his beloved friend Saint Bernard in a passage so sweet and tender that

I commissioned a calligrapher to write it out and then had it framed to celebrate an anniversary with my partner:

> It is in fact a great consolation in this life to have someone to whom you can be united in the intimate embrace of the most sacred love; in whom your spirit can rest; to whom you can pour out your soul; in whose delightful company, as in a sweet consoling song, you can take comfort in the midst of sadness; in whose most welcome friendly bosom you can find peace in so many worldly setbacks; to whose loving heart you can open as freely as you would to yourself your innermost thoughts; through whose spiritual kisses—as by some medicine—you are cured of the sickness of care and worry; who weeps with you in sorrow, rejoices with you in joy, and wonders with you in doubt; whom you draw by the fetters of love into that inner room of your soul, so that though the body is absent, the spirit is there, and you can confer all alone, the more secretly, the more delightfully; with whom you can rest, just the two of you, in the sleep of peace away from the noise of the world, in the embrace of love, in the kiss of unity, with the sweetness of the Holy Spirit flowing over you; to whom you so join and unite yourself that you mix soul with soul, and two become one.
>
> We can enjoy this in the present with those whom we love not merely with our minds but with our hearts; for some are joined to us more intimately and passionately than others in the lovely bond of spiritual friendship. And lest this sort of sacred love should seem improper to anyone, Jesus himself, in everything like us, patient and compassionate with us in every matter, transfigured it through the expression of his own love: for he allowed one, not all, to recline on his breast as a sign of his special love, so that the virgin head was supported in the flowers of the virgin breast, and the closer they were, the more copiously did the fragrant secrets of the heavenly marriage impart the sweet smell of spiritual chrism to their virgin love.

Although all the disciples were blessed with the sweetness of the greatest love of the most holy master, nonetheless he conceded as a privilege to one alone this symbol of a more intimate love, that he should be called the "disciple whom Jesus loved."[9]

When leading retreats, I enjoy comparing different translations of the Gospel writer John's description of the Last Supper. In the King James Version, "the disciple whom Jesus loved" is "leaning on Jesus' bosom." The Revised Standard Version has it that the Beloved Disciple is "lying close to the breast of Jesus." But the New Revised Standard version describes the Beloved Disciple as simply "reclining next" to Jesus. The Beloved Disciple keeps moving progressively *further away* from Jesus, and I fear that, by the next translation, the disciple will be in the other room! It is possibly a similar discomfort that prompts the NRSV to translate a portion of John 1:18 about Jesus' intimacy with God as "who is close to the Father's heart" when the actual text reads "who is close to the Father's bosom."

United Methodist clergyman and Chicago Theological Seminary professor Theodore Jennings translates John's recounting of the moment when the disciples are asking which of them will betray him:

One of his disciples was lying in Jesus' lap, the one Jesus loved; so Simon Peter nods to this one and says: "Tell, whom is he talking about?" That one, falling back on Jesus' chest says to him: "Lord, who is it?"[10]

Rather than simply reject these views of intimacy of Jesus, whether with Mary Magdalene or with John, as heretical, perhaps we can at least understand them as correctives to our own childlike and somewhat naive views of a Jesus without sexual desire. To me what's important in Jesus' close encounters with men and women was that he wasn't concerned with appearance; he wasn't afraid to be thought either straight or gay or sexual. Nor did he fear intimacy. Scripture tells us that he was not concerned if others thought of him as "a glutton and a drunkard." Why would we think Jesus would be offended if we thought of him as sexual? If he was "tempted in every way as we are," we can then better be inspired by his chastity, his singlemindedness of heart and purity of purpose to submit his sexual desires to his responsibility of proclaiming, in word and deed, the transformation needed to embrace the inbreaking commonwealth of God.

Guided by Christ's Values

Given a fresh understanding of Jesus as sexual, though chaste, we might then begin to consider how Christ would express himself sexually, so we might be guided by his values. His notion of the equality of women and men, implied by his response to the questions of divorce and adultery, plus his own apparent regard for women disciples, would commend mutuality and equality of the partners of any sexual relationship. Given his admonitions against hierarchy ("call no man 'father'" . . .; "the first shall be last . . .") one partner would not dominate the other—thus Paul's understanding that the man be head of the wife (1 Corinthians 11:3) must be questioned by Jesus' standards.

That a couple become "one flesh," again a teaching of Jesus from the context of divorce, is echoed in Paul's understanding, progressive for the time, that the man must therefore care for the woman's body as his own, and vice versa. This is progressive because women had been treated as possessions. Paul carries the concept of "one flesh" a step further to define sexual sin, *porneia*, declaring that this principle precludes joining oneself to another in an exploitive sexual relationship. If Paul is consistent in dispensing with purity laws, then we have to imagine this prohibition does not come from a sex worker's "unclean" state, nor from the economic relationship (as all marriages of the time were a matter of economics), but from the lack of mutuality inherent in the relationship, which may mean exploitation, domination, and abuse. It would also imply a lack of both fidelity and chastity on the part of the man, if married. We cannot imagine Jesus behaving so irresponsibly.

In my personal and my pastoral experience, I find mutuality in a relationship is most difficult to gauge and requires time to discover and refine, which argues for courtship. After his "courtship" with his disciples, Jesus could affirm a greater mutuality: "I do not call you servants any longer . . . but I have called you friends" (John 15:15). Jesus' relationship is sacrificial, for, a few verses earlier he declares, "No one has greater love than this, to lay down one's life for one's friends." He prays a few chapters later for his disciples "that they may all be one. As you, Father, are in me and I am in you, may they also be in us . . ." (John 17:21). Finally, he promises a home together for his family of faith, "I go to prepare a place for you, I will come again and will take you to myself, so that where I am, there you may be also." Courtship, mutuality, sacrificial love, unity, and making a home characterized Jesus in his relationships; thus, as his body, they must characterize our relationships. But these are *nonsexual* relationships, you might say.

Some ethicists have questioned the need for specifically sexual ethics, as if this area of our lives is particularly fraught with danger and needs special restraints. Rather, these ethicists suggest that we need an ethic that applies across the board to all of our relationships. Jesus showed us how to live in relationship, by teaching and example. He may not have had a sexual relationship, but he showed us *how* to have sexual relationships as his body.

And "one flesh" involves more than marriage. In blending as "one flesh" Jewish and Gentile Christians, as described in Ephesians, Paul depicts Christ offering a paradigm for the blending of radically different categories of Christians: "in his flesh he has made both groups into one and has broken down the dividing wall, that is, the hostility between us. He has abolished the law with its commandments and ordinances, that he might create in himself one new humanity in place of the two, thus making peace, and might reconcile both groups to God in one body through the cross, thus putting to death that hostility through it" (Ephesians 2:14–16). For our purposes, straight and gay Christians are one in the Body of Christ. Surely if we can share in something as holy and sacred as Christ's body, we can share in something as holy and sacred as marriage.

Making Love as the Body of Christ

Though "making love" has become a euphemism for sexual intercourse, I use it here to mean the *work* of love. Previously I defined lovemaking as *the making of love through caring and commitment as well as touch.* This is the love that Jesus preached and practiced, and it models an ethic that may be applied to all relationships and all commitments, including sexual ones and, specifically, marriage.

Love is a feeling, yes, but love is also a choice, a choice in the moment and a choice for the future. The feeling may lead to the choice to "work things out" to make a future. But the choice to love may also lead to the feeling of love, as it often does in arranged marriages in other cultures. Based on copies requested, the most popular sermon I gave during my ten years at the West Hollywood Presbyterian Church was entitled "Making Love."[11] It took its title from that of a popular film of the time about a married couple who are forced by circumstances to do the work of love when the wife discovers her husband is gay. They are unable to "save" the marriage, but they are able to find ways of continuing to express their committed love as friends. The wife is particularly hard-pressed because loving for her means letting go of her husband.

I gave the sermon because of multiple requests by gay and lesbian couples for guidance, which speaks well of our desire to "get it right" when it comes to relationships. Initially, in ministry within the gay community, I was hesitant to offer any counsel that sounded like "musts" and "shoulds" by which LGBT people have too frequently been battered by fellow Christians, and sometimes by our own political leaders. I also did not consider myself an expert on relationships. As is my wont, I searched through scripture for characteristics of love worthy of imitation. God's covenant relationship, first with Israel, then opened to the whole world through Jesus, provided a model, I believed, for marriage—and a marriage that was no longer intended to be exclusive and isolationist and "nuclear," but one intended to be inclusive of family, friends, neighbors, community, even strangers, like Abraham and Sarah entertaining angels unawares. There was of course historical precedent in Reformed theology, as the marriage covenant was, in John Calvin's view, among God, the community, and the marriage partners.

I have noted that courtship, mutuality, sacrificial love, unity, and homemaking were all part of Jesus' love for his disciples, then and now, and may serve as examples of what is needed in marriage today, regardless of gender-mix. There are three other characteristics for relationships modeled in God's covenantal love for us throughout the Bible that I highlighted in that sermon: *steadfast love* which requires both *faithful-ness* and *forgiveness*. Faithfulness and forgiveness are manifestations of steadfast love and are interrelated. Often the forgiveness most required of partners in a marriage is simply to forgive the other partner for not fulfilling all of our expectations and hopes for the "perfect mate." Additionally, almost inevitably the mercy required of marriage partners is to forgive one another for not being perfected in love.

Henri Nouwen pointed out that all human love falls short of our "first love," how 1 John describes the love of God for us. No human being can ever love us as well, as completely, as long, and as uncondi-tionally as God. God's steadfast love is always there for us, no matter what. God is faithful to us even when we prove unfaithful. And God forgives us our inability to return the love as steadfastly and faithfully and perfectly. Reaching perfection in love is our goal but not our des-tiny. Pursuing this goal is the process of sanctification in the Christian life. In the words of Thomas Merton, "Love in fact *is* the spiritual life."[12] This will be explored in the following chapter.

When we think of faithfulness in marriage, we often reduce it to monogamy, sexual exclusivity. But faithfulness is more than that, and, depending on the promises exchanged, faithfulness may be other than that. In our sex-negative society, we tend to judge the partner who is *sexually* unfaithful. But what of the partner who is unfaithful in other ways, letting work or addictions or distractions or compulsions interfere with her or his *spiritual* faithfulness? Even religion, charitable works, and other commitments to family members and friends may get in the way and make the partner feel abandoned. Alongside adultery, abandon-ment came to be seen as a legitimate reason for divorce, and it is possible for a spouse to "abandon" a partner and family even without physically leaving. "This people honors me with their lips, but their hearts are far from me," Jesus quotes Isaiah regarding perfunctory rituals (Matthew 15:8; Isaiah 29:13). Just as religious displays do not "cover" for an empty heart, externals do not make a marriage; internal disposition does. Historically, the mere *intent* to marry signified the reality.[13]

In my book *Coming Out as Sacrament* and other writings I have devoted many words to another religious display that may cover an empty heart, one found in Paul's description of Communion in 1 Corinthians 11:17–32, particularly his judgment that one who "eats the bread or drinks the cup of the Lord in an unworthy manner will be answerable for the body and blood of the Lord" (verse 27). Paul explains what he means by "in an unworthy manner" in verse 29: "For all who eat and drink *without discerning the body*, eat and drink judgment against themselves" (emphasis mine). At first glance, the reader might think Paul is referring to recipients who do not discern the bread as the body and the cup as the blood of Christ. But most commentators interpret that, in the context of Paul's reprimand about how the meal is distributed in Corinth, the reference instead is to the people gathered as the Body of Christ. Thus "discerning the body" refers to recognizing one another as Christ's body—in a sense, receiving without such discernment is to perform an empty ritual such as Jesus decried when quoting Isaiah.

However the text is interpreted, I believe there is a parallel here to how marriage partners (or sexual partners) may occasion sin when failing to recognize one another as holy, sacred, and beloved children of God and for Christians, as the Body of Christ. Not only are we as individuals the body of Christ reaching out in love, but the recipients of our touch carry the *imago dei*, the image of God, and for Christians, the semblance of Christ. If, in our lovemaking, we fail to discern that we are touching the *imago dei* or the body of Christ—at best, we miss the divine in doing so; at worst, we may disrespect the other's body. For those who are Christian, this does not require a "believer" as a partner when we remember the earlier traditional four-fold experience of Christ, one being Christ who comes to us in the guise of Stranger. Remember how Saint Francis, in hugging and kissing a leper, encountered Christ unawares.

Lovemaking is the making of love through caring and commitment as well as touch. We know about caring. We know about touch. What is commitment? "Commitment is our way of trying to give a future to a present love," Sister Margaret Farley, a Roman Catholic ethicist, writes in *Personal Commitments*.[14] Marriage is a way of making such a commitment. And like many of our commitments, what is most personal and most intimate is celebrated in community. Think of receiving baptism and Communion, or responding to an altar call, or even the simple act of rendering a prayer in worship—all acts of intimacy usually performed in public.

Reflecting on our need to grow in love, Farley clarifies, "Commitment, therefore, is love's way of being whole when it is not yet whole, love's way of offering its incapacities as well as its power."[15] We do not have to be perfect or perfected in love to enter into marriage. Anyone may do so. We do not have to fit some external standard or category; rather, what comes from the heart is what is spiritually vital, as Jesus said. The marriage commitment is not determined by Genesis, gender, or genitals. The Lord looks on the heart, whether speaking of Lord Yahweh or Lord Jesus. Christians might lift their gaze and do the same.

Suffering and Rejoicing Together

The AIDS crisis taught the church much about the need to "suffer with" (the literal meaning of compassion) the gay community, causing many Christians to examine their taboos about sexuality, the stranger, sickness, and death in the process. This was a transforming moment for many people of faith, opening their eyes not only to the suffering related to HIV/AIDS, but also the suffering related to inequality, hate crimes, and inaccessibility to the ministry or to marriage. These so transformed have become supporters and even advocates for our rights in the church and in the world.

Yet some other Christians today may proudly point to their work with AIDS populations and feel that their work is complete. They have accepted that "the Body of Christ has AIDS" without accepting that the Body of Christ also has LGBT members who deserve civil rights, LGBT ministers called to serve, and same-gender couples committed to marriage.

All of these Christians have gotten half of Paul's equation (1 Corinthians 12:26) that, if one member of the body of Christ suffers, all suffer together. But many have failed to "get" the other half of the equation, that if one member of the body is honored, all rejoice together. Many are willing to be there for us when we are sick or dying or dead, but are not as willing to be there for us to celebrate when we are called to ministry or marriage. They cannot bring themselves to rejoice with us in our ordinations and weddings. And that is a serious spiritual failing. It suggests half-heartedness in their welcome and in their outreach. And the Lord looks on the heart. "If I give away all my possessions, and if I hand over my body so that I may boast, but do not have love, I gain nothing" (1 Corinthians 13:3). This verse is in the famous love chapter that immediately follows Paul's exhortation about suffering and rejoicing together as the Body of Christ.

One of the wonders of the Body of Christ is that it is no longer simply associated with a first-century Palestinian Jewish unmarried male living under Roman occupation and rebelling against religious laws of ritual and purity. Now the Body of Christ is from every nation, in every era since Christ, of every hue and ethnicity, either celibate, chaste, or sexually active, in every marital and family arrangement, having a range of disabilities, ages, sexual orientations, and gender identities, of every political persuasion and answerable to every form of government, of every economic and educational class, homeless to propertied, and of varying opinions on the Christian religion—well, you get the picture. This may be why congregational meetings last so long! The diversity of the community of believers over time has prompted any number of changes to doctrines, liturgies, sacraments, biblical interpretations, evangelism, and mission.

In our present time, this diversity includes lesbian, gay, bisexual, and transgender people, whether we are welcoming of them or not. In times past we scapegoated those who did not fit our expectations of "the way things should be"—excommunicating them, sending them off into the wilderness of the secular, cut off from "our" sacraments and "our" churches. Some of "them" have started their own churches, which totally abrogates our rejection of them as Christians. Some of "them" are members of our biological family, so that the wilderness is sometimes only of the heart. And some of "them" have the audacity to refuse to leave, either preaching from "our" pulpits, teaching in "our" seminaries, sitting in "our" pews, or standing just outside "our" church doors. "These people" are not going to go away.

And many who want them to go away are, at the same time, afraid they will. Because many Christians define their faith by what they oppose, yes—but also because there is something in our conscience as followers of Jesus Christ that tells us that LGBT people need to be in church too. So we devise ways that they can conform to our standards, at least our standards for them, our double standards that we would never apply to ourselves: celibacy, or marriage to a gender for which they do not yearn, marriage to someone they cannot love, or, for transgender people, not being outwardly the gender they are inwardly.

Meanwhile, not only our community has changed—at least in the sense that now some LGBT people can be out of the closet—our community's beliefs are changing. People who are happily heterosexually married are questioning why we would limit God's creativity, compassion, and community to straight people. They are wondering why marriage couldn't be for same-gender couples, why LGBT people couldn't be ordained. They are even debating whether *anti*-gay people belong in the church! Though Jesus never spoke directly against slavery, the Body of Christ has. Though Jesus never spoke directly against racism and sexism, the Body of Christ has. And though Jesus never addressed homophobia directly, the Body of Christ can.

And so our spirituality is changing. Some of us resist this with anchors called "fundamentals" such as biblical literalism, dogmatic certainties, "inerrant" church pronouncements, or simply "the way things should be." Yet throughout the centuries, Holy Spirit, sent from Christ, has led us out of our comfort zones, opening our safe sanctuaries to people different from us, changing the rules that exclude in favor of an inclusive evangelism, redefining boundaries as to what it means to be Christian. And just when we do open ourselves to "these people" whom we have comfortably viewed from a judgmental distance, it's even more threatening to find out that they are much like us: Christians, ministers, married, and parents!

Jesus at a Wedding in California

I end this chapter on sex and the Body of Christ revisiting a *midrash* I wrote on Jesus attending the wedding at Cana in John, chapter two. It first appeared in my second book, *Come Home! Reclaiming Spirituality and Community as Gay Men and Lesbians.*[16] I revised it for the sermon described at the beginning of this book, a sermon following the trial of a member of the Body of Christ for performing a same-gender wedding.

> Now there was a same-gender wedding at a church in California, and Jesus was there. When the wine ran out, Jesus' mother asked him to do something about it. Jesus rolled his eyes, smiled, and said, "Mom, this isn't the right time!" Nonetheless, Jesus' mother told the caterers to do whatever he asked them to do. Not long after, Jesus told them to fill the baptismal font with water and to serve the guests from it. When the caterers began to draw from the baptismal, they discovered that what came out was an exquisite cabernet for those wanting red wine, a very fine chardonnay for those preferring white wine, and tasty grape juice for those desiring a non-alcoholic alternative. Everyone was amazed at the miracle, and they realized something eternal had surfaced in that moment.
>
> But news reports of Jesus' miracle at a same-gender marriage angered religious people throughout the country. Leaders of the religious right claimed Jesus' action had been misunderstood, blamed the media who reported it, and condemned the church for fabricating the story. Mainstream liberal churches issued a statement that it was not much of a miracle or else the caterers would have been able to serve a blush wine as well. A little miffed and jealous, even progressive congregations complained, demanding to know why Jesus hadn't done the same thing at civil unions in their churches! And at the Vatican, a special conclave of cardinals demanded the pope's resignation. Exasperated, the pope asked why. "Because," he was told, "If you can't control Jesus Christ, how can we expect you to control the church?!"[17]

Ultimately the question of same-gender marriage will be resolved when we as the Body of Christ, the church, allow the Spirit of Christ to lead us where some fear to go.

Notes

[1] Chris Glaser, *Uncommon Calling: A Gay Christian's Struggle to Serve the Church*, expanded edition (Louisville, KY: Westminster John Knox Press, 1988 and 1996), 224.

[2] Joseph Kaster, *Putnam's Concise Mythological Dictionary* (New York: Capricorn Books, 1964), 61.

[3] Byron Shafer, *The Church and Homosexuality*, the Background Paper of the Task Force to Study Homosexuality, received as a study document by the 190th General Assembly (1978) of The United Presbyterian Church in the United States of America, 22.

[4] This is my own interpretation of this passage. The actual phrase is that a Christian becomes one flesh with "a prostitute" and thus Christ would be one flesh with a prostitute—an unthinkable proposition in Paul's view. But, considering Jesus' own defenses of the woman accused of adultery and of women divorced by men and thus economically cut off, I believe that Jesus would be more concerned with sexual exploitation than with blaming the victim of economic limitations. And in particular, women in Israel were not allowed to earn their own income through conventional means.

[5] Boswell, *Same-Sex Unions*, 219–220, footnote 4.

[6] Countryman, *Dirt, Greed, and Sex*, 210.

[7] Marcus J. Borg, *Meeting Jesus Again for the First Time: The Historical Jesus and the Heart of Contemporary Faith* (San Francisco: HarperSanFrancisco, 1994).

[8] Glaser, *Come Home!*, 37–44.

[9] Boswell, *Christianity, Social Tolerance, and Homosexuality*, 225–226.

[10] Theodore Jennings, *The Man Jesus Loved: Homoerotic Narratives from the New Testament* (Cleveland, OH: Pilgrim Press, 2003), 16.

[11] A version of this sermon can be found in my book *Come Home!* cited above, Chapter 12; "Making Love."

[12] Thomas Merton, *The Wisdom of the Desert: Sayings from the Desert Fathers of the Fourth Century* (New York: New Directions Books, 1960), 17.

[13] Witte, *From Sacrament to Contract*, 28.

[14] Margaret A. Farley, *Personal Commitments: Beginning, Keeping, Changing* (San Francisco: Harper & Row, 1986), 40.

[15] Farley, *Personal Commitments*, 134.

[16] Glaser, *Come Home!*, 116.

[17] Adapted from Chapter 15 "Dwelling in Beulah Land," in *Come Home!*, second edition (Chapter 15 added to original Harper & Row edition, 1990), 116.

꧁꧂

CHAPTER SIX

As My Own Soul

Marriage as a Spiritual Discipline

And it came to pass . . . that the soul of Jonathan was knit with the soul of David, and Jonathan loved him as his own soul.
— 1 Samuel 18:1, KJV

Now . . . those who believed were of one heart and soul, and no one claimed private ownership of any possessions, but everything they owned was held in common.
— Acts 4:32

Love Stories

The whole of the Bible could be said to be the story of what God did for love.[1] But within that story are multiple love stories. The Song of Solomon is a collection of poems presented in dialogue form that sensually celebrates the love of a man and a woman, with only one reference to marriage (3:11). Over the centuries interpreters have sought to spiritualize the sexually charged exchanges, suggesting the love story is a metaphor for the relationship of God and Israel or Christ and his church, but the "plain sense" of the text is clear. These lovers are hot for one another, and poetically describe body parts and physical intimacy that would make "the kindly old grandmother" that I worried about in Chapter Five blush. The book is also known as the Song of Songs, a Hebrew phrase suggesting its superlative nature, like "King of Kings."[2] The yearning of its lovers and their passion may be summed up in these elevated and eloquent verses:

> Set me as a seal upon your heart,
>   as a seal upon your arm;
> for love is strong as death,
>   passion fierce as the grave.
> Its flashes are flashes of fire,
>   a raging flame.
> Many waters cannot quench love,
>   neither can floods drown it.
> If one offered for love
>   all the wealth of his house,
>   it would be utterly scorned.
>   (Song of Solomon 8:6–7)

A seminary classmate with whom I shared this yearning sent me these words in a stressful period of absence from one another. I heard them as if for the first time.

Previously I mentioned that early Christians did not explain the sacraments of baptism or Communion until a catechumen had first received them, believing that participation was key to comprehending their sacred nature and true meaning. In the same way, I could not have understood these verses my boyfriend sent without first experiencing the reality within them. "You had to be there," we might say of an experience we can't quite convey in words. This could be said of the mystical experiences recounted in scripture as well. But once I had firsthand experience that "love is as strong as death" the words resonated within me, even if I had to translate them from the context of an opposite-gender relationship.

I earlier wrote that same-gender couples have more experience "translating" the stories of opposite-gender couples into our own relationships. But that is not to say that heterosexual people have no experience translating same-gender experience, if only in their imagination.

I was touched when my father, in a theoretical conversation over dinner about homosexuality before I came out to my parents, told my mother, "If they feel for each other what I feel for you, I can understand why they want their relationships."[3]

And many opposite-gender weddings incorporate the vows that one woman made to another:

> Entreat me not to leave you
>   or to return from following you;
> for where you go I will go,
>   and where you lodge I will lodge;
> your people shall be my people,
>   and your God my God;
> where you die, I will die,
>   and there will I be buried.
> May the Lord do so to me and more also
>   if even death parts me from you.
>   (Ruth 1:16–17, RSV)

Ruth said this to her mother-in-law Naomi in the Book of Ruth, a love story that depicts how two women managed to survive against all odds by sticking together. Naomi and her husband moved to Moab, but her husband died, leaving her with two sons. Naomi's sons married Moabite daughters, Orpah and Ruth, but the sons died childless. Naomi decides to return to her family in Bethlehem in Judah, and urges the daughters to stay in Moab to find husbands. Orpah stayed, but Ruth "clung" to Naomi, reciting these vows. In them, Ruth promises everything marriage does: to follow Naomi anywhere, to live together, to become part of her family and a resident of her country, to embrace her religion, to live as one "till death do us part" and to be buried with her. And her vow invokes Yahweh, as she would have ritually made a chopping gesture to her neck as she speaks the words, "May the Lord do so to me and more also if even death parts me from you."

Their economic circumstances as women in their era and their culture required that one of them find marriage to a male, as they would not have been permitted to have their own income. Ruth was the most likely candidate, being a woman of child-bearing age. And so they maneuver Ruth into a marriage with Boaz, a relative of Naomi's husband. When Ruth produces an heir, their women friends gather round Naomi and thank God that the child "will be to you a restorer of life and a nourisher of your old age; for your daughter-in-law who loves you, who is more to you than seven sons, has borne him." And Naomi becomes the infant's wet-nurse. The son's descendants will include King David and ultimately, Jesus.

Was Ruth and Naomi's relationship a marriage? Well, not a marriage that would have been recognized by "the powers that be" of their time. Neither was male, no woman was owned, no bride price was paid, and procreation would have been impossible without their ingenuity of finding a sperm donor. And we know as little about whether their "marriage" was consummated as we would of any childless opposite-gender couple. But, in my view, this is not the point. The point is that spiritually their relationship had the attributes of a marriage.

The same could be said of the relationship of their descendant, David, and Saul's son, Jonathan. Much of 1 and 2 Samuel is devoted to this epic tale of handsome protagonists, royal family drama, military valor, political intrigue, colossal battles, and tender love scenes. If Ruth and Naomi would make a great "chick flick," the story of Saul and David and Jonathan would make a great "guy flick." Except that the tender loves scenes are between David and Jonathan, and the scenes of jealousy are played out by Saul and, behind the scenes, Yahweh "himself."

At least two strands of the story are interwoven in the text, evidenced by a lack of continuity as to when Saul actually comes to know David. It starts "once upon a time" when God's people favor having a human king over a theocracy—displacing a jealous Yahweh. The prophet Samuel is led to anoint Saul, "a handsome young man." In workshops on "Outing the Bible" and her book *Our Tribe*, the Rev. Nancy Wilson, now Moderator of Metropolitan Community Churches, suggests a "gay sensibility" in the physical descriptions of the leading men in this legendary story, unusual for the Bible. Of Saul it is said, "There was not a man among the people of Israel more handsome than he; he stood head and shoulders above everyone else" (1 Samuel 9:2). "There is no one like him among all the people," Samuel declares (10:23).

But when Saul in turn is displaced as king for abrogating God's bloodthirsty demands and ritual requirements, made through Samuel (yes, that's *another* story!), David is described as even more winsome when Samuel anoints him as boy-who-would-be-king: "Now he was ruddy, and had beautiful eyes, and was handsome." Even the bruiser Philistine Goliath, ten feet tall and able to carry the weight of more than 150 pounds of armor, with a spear whose head weighed 19 pounds, is described as recognizing his opponent as "a youth, ruddy and hand-some in appearance" (17:42).

There are tender scenes between Saul, now afflicted by "an evil spirit"—perhaps mental illness—and David, who "entered his service. Saul loved him greatly, and he became his armor-bearer. . . . And whenever the evil spirit from God came upon Saul, David took the lyre and played it with his hand, and Saul would be relieved and feel better, and the evil spirit would depart from him" (16:21, 23). But even more intimate is the scene in which Jonathan lays eyes on David for the first time:

> When David had finished speaking to Saul, the soul of Jonathan was bound ["knit" in the KJV] to the soul of David, and Jonathan loved him as his own soul. . . . Then Jonathan made a covenant with David, because he loved him as his own soul. Jonathan stripped himself of the robe that he was wearing, and gave it to David, and his armor, and even his sword and his bow and his belt. (1 Samuel 18:1, 3–4)

Two men exchanging armor or clothes would have been an outward sign of the invisible reality of their friendship, a ritual common in ancient times to seal a covenant. But what is extraordinary to me is the unilateral gesture of Jonathan stripping himself and surrendering his defenses and weaponry out of love for David. This would be paralleled by his decision not to fight to inherit his father's throne but to support David as king. Previously mentioned, Saul would jealously rage at Jonathan, "You son of a perverse, rebellious woman! Do I not know that you have chosen the son of Jesse [David] to your own shame, and the shame of your mother's nakedness? For as long as the son of Jesse lives upon the earth, neither you nor your kingdom shall be established" (20:30–31). Using the epithet of "the shame of your mother's nakedness" carries a sexual connotation. In his father's eyes, Jonathan has given up his manhood out of love for David.

David may have loved Jonathan, too, but Jonathan gushed over David: "Jonathan took great delight in David" (19:1c). "Jonathan spoke well of David . . ." (19:4). "Then Jonathan said to David, 'Whatever you say, I will do for you'" (20:4). "Jonathan made David swear again by his love for him; for he loved him as he loved his own life" (20:17).

Honoring his father the king, Jonathan would fight in Saul's army. A time comes when Jonathan and David must bid one another farewell, and they arrange a secret rendezvous out hunting reminiscent of *Brokeback Mountain*:

> David arose out of a place toward the south, and fell on his face to the ground, and bowed himself three times: and they kissed one another, and wept one with another, until David exceeded. And Jonathan said to David, Go in peace, forasmuch as we have sworn both of us in the name of the Lord, saying, "The Lord be between me and thee, and between my seed and thy seed for ever." And he arose and departed: and Jonathan went into the city. (1 Samuel 20:41–42, KJV)

Notice in the King James Version quoted here the tenderness of the kissing and tears. Note too that the ambiguity of the English translation "David exceeded" is in the Hebrew text as well, leading biblical scholar Tom Horner, in one of the earliest books on homosexuality and the Bible, to find there a sexual connotation.[4] But of greater interest to me is how differently subsequent translations have treated this intimate passage, much like the squeamish extrication of the Beloved Disciple from Jesus' bosom.

In the Revised Standard Version, there is kissing and tears, but the last phrase is rendered as "until David recovered himself" which is very different from "until David exceeded," which now is found as an alternative translation in a footnote. The New Revised Standard Version translates it as "David wept the more," which captures the meaning of excess, with a footnote saying the meaning of the Hebrew text is uncertain. The

New Jerusalem Bible translates the entire verse as "then they embraced each other, both weeping copiously." The Modern Language version reads, "They kissed each other and wept together until David got control of himself." The Living Bible butches up the passage considerably, saying nothing about David prostrating himself in front of Jonathan, or bowing three times, or them kissing one another, but describes them stoically: "and they sadly shook hands, tears running down their cheeks until David could weep no more." The Living Bible then follows this understated drama by translating Jonathan's "Go in peace" as "Cheer up"! I have a feeling that a future translation of this verse will have David and Jonathan texting one another goodbye from opposite ends of the field: "cya."

All of this is to say that, whatever the nature of Jonathan and David's relationship, we in the twenty-first century have a transmission problem in knowing for certain. Just as the experience of other marginalized people was filtered out by the myopia or outright prejudice of biblical writers, scribes, translators, and interpreters, so the experience of LGBT people has been ignored, disguised, rejected, or forgotten. In fairness, those responsible for our sacred texts did not have our present understanding of sexual orientation and gender identity, and simply excluded or judged LGBT experience as impure, unnatural, sinful, or unworthy of historical memory. Regardless, we are blessed in the stories of Ruth and Naomi and Jonathan and David to have insights into the spirituality of every relationship, from friendship to marriage. No opposite-gender marriage or friendship is described in such intimate detail in all of scripture.

David married twenty wives, including Jonathan's sister Michal, for whom he was required to pay a most unusual brideprice: one hundred Philistine foreskins! He engaged in the requisite adulterous affair, and had concubines besides. But the love and friendship between David and Jonathan fit the standards we would want in a marriage by invoking God in their love of each other and the promise of protection of their respective progeny found in Jonathan's parting words, "Go in peace, since both of us have sworn in the name of the Lord, saying, 'The Lord shall be between me and you, and between my descendants and your descendants forever'" (20:42). And David subsequently proved faithful to this covenant when he came to the rescue of Jonathan's son with a disability (2 Samuel 9). Just a generation or two ago in the United States, this kind of relationship on the side was the most two men could expect.

Jonathan was killed defending his father's honor. When David learned of it, he tore his clothes, mourned, wept, and fasted all day. His elegiac reply, recorded at the beginning of 2 Samuel, resonates with all those who have loved someone as their own soul:

> How the mighty have fallen
>   in the midst of the battle!
> Jonathan lies slain upon your high places.
> I am distressed for you, my brother Jonathan;
>   greatly beloved were you to me;
>   your love to me was wonderful,
>   passing the love of women.
>   (2 Samuel 1:25–26)

Not too much should be made of David's declaration that Jonathan's love surpassed that of women, as women and their love were not as valued as men and their love in those times. Even today, men who have served in battle together enjoy a love and an intimacy unique to the experience of standing shoulder to shoulder in dangerous circumstances. But I have also found this "band of brothers" experience may be had among gay and bisexual and transgender men who have withstood together the risks of rejection, discrimination, hatred, violence, and AIDS. Lesbian and bisexual and transgender women similarly enjoy a unique sisterhood, having faced together sexism, misogyny, inequality, violence, and cancer.

The early Christians knew this experience as well. Having endured the trial and torture and crucifixion of their beloved leader and persecutions themselves, the ridicule of their belief in his resurrection and their experience of Holy Spirit, and the opposition of "the powers that be" to the reign of God they saw breaking into the world, believers too were said to be "of one heart and soul, and no one claimed private ownership of any possessions, but everything they owned was held in common" (Acts 4:32).

The lovers of the Song of Solomon bespeak a passion that cannot be quenched. Ruth and Naomi witness a desire to share a common life. Jonathan yearns to sacrificially love and care for another, David, as his very own soul. And the early Christians, in the midst of adversity and persecutions, are of one heart and soul, sharing their belongings with one another.

These are the graces to be found in marriage: passion, a common life, sacrificial care, sharing resources. That these graces are celebrated in stories I've selected from the Bible that, respectively, depict sexual union, two same-gender love relationships, and lastly, spiritual union, is quite intentional. I believe these are also the graces to be found in both our spiritual life and in our sexuality: passion, a common life, sacrificial care, and sharing resources. In much of Christian history, the spiritual life and spiritual community have been predicated on a rejection of the earthly, of the body, of sexuality, even of marriage. But if we were to imagine that the inbreaking commonwealth of God is, rather, sex-positive, embodied, and a pro-earthly experience, how vital marriage could be as a location for spiritual growth, intimacy and ecstasy, compassion and abundant hospitality! This is what contemporary Christian body theologians, of whom Jim Nelson is one, write about, reclaiming the valuing of the body in Christian thought.

What if we viewed marriage as a form of spiritual training rather than "a remedy for sin," a place to discern what it means to be human, loving, and holy? What if we defined marriage not by whom it excluded but by the attributes of steadfast love, faithfulness, and forgiveness? What if we considered marriage a calling, a vocation, by which anyone may "glorify God and enjoy God forever"? What if we recognized that marriage's gift to the world is not a narrow fertility but a broader fecundity? And what if we followed our conscience to listen to the child of reason and experience—science—when it confirms that there are spectrums of sexual orientation and gender identity, not only among human beings but among all creatures, making sexual and gender diversity quite natural, part of the created order? If we were to do all of this, we would be blessed with a spirituality of marriage independent of outward appearances, exclusivity, and scapegoating. We would be looking on the heart of a marriage, as the Lord does, regarding a marriage by the content of its character rather than by the gender of its partners.

The Spirituality of Marriage, Regardless of Gender

What follows is a brief analysis of Christian attitudes toward marriage that John Witte, Jr. discusses in greater detail in his comprehensive book, *From Sacrament to Contract: Marriage, Religion, and Law in the Western Tradition* already cited. The condensation and many of the conclusions I draw from the material are my own, however, and all conclusions in relation to same-gender marriage are mine.

John Chrysostom (345–407) observed that if marriage was wrong, Paul would never have compared Christ to a bridegroom and the church to his bride. "This, then, is what it means to marry in Christ: spiritual marriage is like spiritual birth," he wrote.[5] And while Augustine of Hippo (354–430), like others, viewed marriage as a way to cope with lust, he saw the union in marriage as compensation for the loss of communion with the Creator in Eden.[6] These several views serve as positive spiritual foundations for marriage in early Christianity. Despite Paul's "default" attitude regarding marriage ("better than to burn"), he uses marriage as a model for the church's communion with Christ, as does the visionary John in "the marriage of the Lamb" in Revelation. Chrysostom's concept that marriage is "like spiritual birth" gives marriage a baptismal connotation, as baptism marks a Christian's spiritual birth. Augustine's notion that sexual union in marriage is a kind of substitute for spiritual union with God elevates marriage as well.

The earliest Christian understanding of marriage as a sacrament viewed the marriage partners as "ministers of the sacrament," whose mere exchange of promises afforded the efficacy of the sacrament, requiring no overt church involvement unlike the six other sacraments then recognized.[7] Marriage served like other sacraments as a channel of sanctification that blessed participants with God's grace, transforming marriage partners as baptism did. "The most startling feature of the sacrament was that it transformed sexual intercourse from an otherwise sinful act of lust into a spiritual act of great symbolic value," Witte explains. The transformation guaranteed God's help, "welcoming them into the hierarchy of institutions that comprised the church universal."[8]

Precedent, then, suggests that same-gender marriage, like opposite-gender marriage, does not require church approval to be efficacious as a sacrament—all that is needed are the ministers of the sacrament, the marriage partners themselves. Same-gender marriage may also serve as a channel of sanctification that blesses the partners with God's transforming grace. And, most striking, as it was believed that heterosexual intercourse was a "sinful act of lust" that could be transformed into "a spiritual act of great symbolic value" by marriage, so, even if Christians view homosexual intercourse negatively, it too would thus be transformed. The Reformer John Calvin would subsequently teach that the moral standing of the celebrant of *any* sacrament would not affect its efficacy, which serves to strengthen this argument of the efficacy of same-gender marriage as sacramental.

Traditionalists might be shocked by my argument. They would say, no, that marriage is sacramental because of its association with Christ's marriage with his bride, the church. If this metaphor is interpreted literally, then it's true that same-gender marriages could not represent such male-female duality—except in the metaphorical sense of masculine/feminine complementarity of any two people who come together, share a household, and divide responsibilities. But if we take the metaphor of Christ and his church literally, what of the other biblical metaphor of the church as the Body of Christ? If the church is also the Body of Christ, would not then Christ be marrying himself? Taken another way, the Body of Christ now consists of a great diversity of people—would that make of Christ a polygamist? These ludicrous examples demonstrate the folly of understanding this metaphor literally.

Just as LGBT people have been able to translate heterosexual romance and relationships to our own experience, so the church requires imagination enough to view same-gender marriages as parallel in kind to opposite-gender marriages. Frankly, I believe that *much more* imagination is required to view Christ and his church's consummation of their relationship as a wedding! Even more so if taken literally!

What Witte says of the first Christian marriages could be said of our latter day same-gender Christian marriages: "To declare such marriages 'nonsacramental' was tantamount to removing them from the spiritual jurisdiction and sacramental care of the church."[9] Can we imagine Jesus wanting us to exclude same-gender marriages and partners from the blessing and care of his Body?

Martin Luther took issue with just how "natural" church law was when it privileged celibacy and discouraged marriage. He recognized that preventing individuals from marrying who did not have the gift of celibacy could lead to indiscriminate and irresponsible sex.[10] (This has had recent confirmation in a 2008 study of adolescents who pledged abstinence until marriage and those who didn't. Those in the first group had as much pre-marital sex as the second group, but practiced riskier sex.[11]) Marriage was not only a cure for those unable to control themselves, but a duty for those who could, a virtual requirement—no doubt a pendulum that now swung the other way. Luther's concept of a two-kingdom division—one of earth, and one of heaven—is reminiscent of James B. Nelson's pyramid of control presented in Chapter Two that separated heaven from earth, spirit from body, spirituality from sexuality. For Luther, marriage belonged to the earthly kingdom, not the heavenly one, so it was up to the state to oversee marriage, though the state administers on behalf of God. The church's responsibility was to teach God's will for marriage to citizens and their leaders, to provide models of married partners, to maintain a public registry of marriages, and to bless, teach, and correct a couple during their wedding and throughout their marriage.[12]

Though viewing marriage as a duty may seem grim, inherent in this understanding is that marriage is not just for the "weak" or the "sinful," but for the strong and the whole. Today, most Roman Catholics join Protestants in viewing celibacy as a gift, though Roman Catholicism still requires this "gift" for ordained ministry—and we have seen how well that has worked out in recent public scandals and class action lawsuits. Most Christians have ample information that accessibility to marriage at least discourages indiscriminate and irresponsible sex. Ironically, the very criticism once leveled at LGBT people that we did not form long-term attachments is attenuated by our advocacy of same-gender marriage rights. And those who once lobbed this accusation now lobby against same-gender marriage, weakening their self-righteous argument. Many of us would critique Luther's strict duality of heavenly and earthly kingdoms, but others of us would see in it a precursor to our own separation of church and state. If indeed the state should regulate marriage, church teaching may only serve as guidance, not law. For Luther, marriage is not a sacrament. Because marriage is an affair of state, it can readily be argued that it is in the best interests of the state to recognize *all* of its citizens and all institutions such as marriage that benefit its citizenry.

John Calvin came to see a parallel between God's covenant with humanity (first with the children of Israel, then with "the elect" of Christ) and the marriage covenant. The marriage covenant included not only the marriage partners, but also their parents and community leaders, both civil and spiritual—all of whom represented God's presence in the marriage.[13] Though earlier Calvin had associated sexuality, marriage, and family solely with earth, his later writings nuanced the division between earth and heaven into two tracks relevant to marriage: the "morality of duty" expected of all and the "morality of aspiration" expected of believers, separating expectations in marriage of everyone regardless of faith from what may be accomplished spiritually by believers.[14]

The covenant view of marriage supports the necessity of the civil and ecclesiastical embrace of same-gender marriage. The opposing argument goes that the state and the church should not have to accept our "lifestyle"—which, remember, absolutely parallels the heterosexual "lifestyle" in both its vagueness as a term and diversity of expressions. But to enter the covenant of marriage requires all the parties to the covenant—partners, parents, church, and state—to covenant together to uphold the marriage. Calvin's covenant of marriage also gave a comprehensive theory to something Protestant and later Catholic teachers believed (evidenced at the Council of Trent), that marriages should be public. Earlier this was supported by biblical proof texts; now it could be supported by an integrated theology of marriage.[15] So "going public" with same-gender marriages is not a case of "flaunting" but an example of welcoming all parties into their covenants.

Beginning in the seventeenth century, English Puritans and English Catholics alike subscribed to a commonwealth model for marriage, recognizing its religious roots but politicizing marriage "for the common weale" of the Commonwealth of England. As John Witte, Jr. describes it:

> The couple was not merely joining in covenant with each other
> and with God, as Continental Protestants taught. They were not
> merely symbolically representing the mysterious union of Christ

and His Church, as Catholics taught. The couple was also, in effect, joining in covenant with the Church and Commonwealth of England—past, present, and future.[16]

Marriage was thus foundational to the well-being of the greater commonwealth, perhaps the notion that prompts a similar view of many in the United States as an inheritor of the British ethos—that marriage is essential to the well-being of the nation.

The commonwealths of the state, church, and marriage were governed by parallel hierarchies, royals over subjects, clergy over laity, and husband over wife and children. But they were different in that the state wielded legal and military authority, the church controlled Word and Sacrament, and the family managed duty and love.[17] Especially in this period, English writers romanticized about marital love as never before: "Marital love is the highest love, for it is simultaneously spiritual and sensual, Christian and carnal—a sweet compounde of both religion and nature," Daniel Rogers declared in 1642 in *Matrimoniall Honour*.[18]

So same-gender couples were not the first to "politicize marriage"! Of course, marriage had been a political tool in ages past to forge political, economic, and diplomatic alliances among the privileged and between nations. Now it served as the foundational unit for a burgeoning empire. "The personal is political" was the mantra of the modern women's movement because it is true. Just as the Body of Christ includes LGBT people and same-gender marriages, so does the body politic. To grant same-gender couples the same rights and rites as opposite-gender couples does not politicize marriage; rather, the resistance to share these rights by the dominant culture demonstrates the already-existing reality of marriage as an institution of political power and privilege.

Whether regarded as sacrament, social estate, covenant, or commonwealth, Christians affirmed practical considerations of marriage, such as procreation and the rearing of children and ensuring mutual care and protection of the parties involved, including protection from lust. They also reflected the notion that marriage, in its ancient origins, implies a sacred trust as a divinely inspired institution, as "the way things should be"—a belief that even a non-religious person may hold because of its association with the natural. As long as same-gender sexual relations are considered "unnatural," same-gender couples will have difficulty obtaining the right to marry. But once conscience forces our reason to heed its progeny, empirical science, about the naturalness of same-gender sexual relations for those of homosexual and bisexual orientation, as well as the ability of same-gender couples to form families through adoption, insemination, and surrogates, the positive sacred taboo surrounding marriage will come to include same-gender partners, who need the same mutual care and protection for themselves and their families. Ancient historical texts already testify to how far back the existence of same-gender partnerships extend, and this chapter began by illustrating how the Bible itself describes with admiration the character and possibilities of same-gender love in the stories of Ruth and Naomi and Jonathan and David.

Civil Marriage, Not Civil Unions

The Enlightenment of the seventeenth and eighteenth centuries emphasized the choice of the individuals involved, the contractual element of marriage, and this comes closest to what is practiced today in the West. No longer was reason only to be found through religion. No longer was God viewed as arranging "his" schedule around us. Individuals were "created equal in virtue and dignity, vested with inherent rights of life, liberty, and property, and capable of pursuing independent means and measures of happiness without involvement from any other person or institution."[19] Thus, "all men are created equal . . . endowed by their Creator with certain unalienable rights . . . among these are life, liberty and the pursuit of happiness," as Thomas Jefferson wrote in the Declaration of Independence. Enlightenment ideals like these gave rise to our present understanding of civil marriage.

Yet the state (unduly influenced by religion) has interfered with the choice of the individuals involved by refusing same-gender couples the right to marry and our children the right to remain with us. Just as we do not take Jefferson's words literally to mean that *only* men are created equal, but we include women too, there is little reason to take references to a marriage of one man and one woman literally when the language was originally put in place in canons and confessions to limit the *number* of partners in a marriage, not to specify the *genders*.

Many same-gender couples do our best, with the help of lawyers, to establish some semblance of marital and familial contracts with limited protections, yet even these may be challenged by blood relatives and are endangered by the current movement to constitutionalize marriage for opposite-gender partners only. Civilly, this is the area in which there should be the least controversy, because God and church are not involved, although it could be said that the equality of partners in any marriage grows out of religious principles, as does the equality of same-gender marriages with opposite-gender marriages.

Just as we have entered into contracts unique to our situation, many same-gender couples, often with the help of clergy, have created our own nuptials—just as African-American slaves created their own nuptials such as "jumping the broom" when denied marriage ceremonies. Self-determination has been an essential element in Western marriage, where mere intent to marry was regarded as creating the reality, and couples in truth married themselves. In this way same-gender marriages need no validation from either the state or the church, and yet to enjoy the support of either or both augments the intent of the individuals as well as granting them the rights and privileges bestowed on opposite-gender marriages. The federal government's nonpartisan General Accounting Office has calculated that there are 1,149 rights and benefits afforded civil marriage, most of which are denied even those who are allowed civil unions. As discussed in Chapter One, there is no truth in "separate but equal"—so domestic partnerships and civil unions will never be equal to marriage, and the proponents of these lesser arrangements know that, or else we would simply be offered marriage. Now, some of these proponents are well meaning, but they are giving in to one of two unacceptable propositions, either that marriage belongs only to opposite-gender partners, or that the majority thinks this is true and this is the best we can do.

The reader will have noted that throughout this book I have resisted using the term "gay marriage" which I fear, in common parlance, has been used to describe something other than marriage, especially when "straight marriage" is almost never used side by side with "gay marriage."

My preference would be just to talk about marriage, but because, in the minds of many, marriage is a privilege only of opposite-gender partners, I have had to make the distinction of same-gender marriage and opposite-gender marriage to be understood. I look forward to the day when together, we may simply have a conversation about marriage.

As if we don't already know, those who oppose LGBT people frequently remind us that there are social dimensions to any of our "personal" decisions, especially when it comes to marriage. Yet just as we would expect LGBT people to be socially responsible in the conduct of their lives, so LGBT people should expect the majority culture to be socially responsible in its equal application of marriage law. Of great concern presently is the tyranny of the majority who through their "personal" decisions at the polls prevent a minority from marrying. That's why the Civil Rights movement avoided putting African-American equality to a vote of the popular electorate, relying instead on legislatures and courts to defend their rights. Unjust criticism has been made of "activist judges" when they are simply doing their job: interpreting constitutions and laws "blindly," without regard to the outward appearance or condition of those seeking parity, a legal version of the Lord "looking on the heart."

Marriage as Spiritual Opportunity

I don't believe lesbian couples or gay couples do any better at marriage than straight couples. Nor do I believe they do any worse. But I believe that same-gender couples must have the same opportunity to succeed and fail at marriage. Three different pundits have been credited with the quip about marriage for same-gender couples: "Gay people should be just as miserable as we are!" Given the lack of support and the active discrimination same-gender partners face, it's a wonder so many have relatively happy and stable marriages.

Marriage should never become a source of competition, because marriage, in my view, is essentially a spiritual discipline. "Winning" is ultimately by the grace of God, because, as with any spiritual discipline, there is no guarantee of its effects or our efforts, and, speaking from an eternal perspective, there is no "finish line." "Losing" is a cause for grief, but not a loss of personal value, though it may feel that way and others may treat the divorced parties that way.

A spiritual discipline may be understood as a means toward transcendence. Chastity—which simply means purity of heart, purity of purpose—subordinates desire to responsibility, *eros* governed by *agape*. But it's not all about control. Partners in marriage grow closer to God, suggests a 2008 *Newsweek* article on the Bible and same-gender marriage, quoting the Rev. Chloe Breyer, executive director of New York's Interfaith Center: "Being with one another in community is how you love God."[20]

Marital intimacy, loving someone as my own soul, is an occasion for ecstasy—literally, "out of stasis"—being taken out of ourselves, out of the status quo, into a new reality with the lover and the Lover. This transcendence takes us beyond ourselves and into relationship, and, frankly, sometimes *out* of relationships because the passionate "urge to merge," left unchecked, can lead to codependent or abusive or exploitive or simply unhealthy relationships—in both religion and in marriage.

The term "discipline" may have negative connotations, because we often associate the word with punishment and/or a punitive system of education. But if we think of the disciplines of medicine or art or even learning how to ski, we come close to what I intend when I speak of marriage as a spiritual discipline. A spiritual discipline is about focus. One of my favorite lines about the challenge of contemporary relationships from a recent romantic film is, "It's not so much about monogamy—it's about focus." In Christian monastic discipline the goal is "to pray always," exercising awareness of communion with God in every moment. Even so, a Christian marriage discipline may have the challenging goal "to love always," exercising awareness of communion with a partner in every moment. Another way of thinking of focus is the Buddhist practice of mindfulness—in the case of marriage, paying attention to a partner and to your self.

So much of spiritual discipline has been based on sex and body negativity that it's hard to conceive a spiritual discipline based on sex and body positivity. Spiritual disciplines have included fasting, solitariness, sexual abstinence, and flagellation—all to discipline the body so the spirit might rise heavenward to God. Reading the stories of the

Desert Fathers and often forgotten Desert Mothers, as well as the lives of saints and rules of monastic communities, I must confess that, while deeply appreciative of most of their spiritual disciplines and spiritual insights, I flinch at the harsher instances of self-denial and self-abuse. To their credit, the greatest spiritual teachers discouraged overdoing it, recognizing unhealthy behaviors as well as fearing spiritual pride. A cause for empathy is that some monastics probably refused or left marriages to avoid brutality, domination, or heterosexual expectations. As John Boswell, occasionally given to hyperbole, used to joke, "Why wouldn't a gay man want to become a priest in the Middle Ages, when it immediately introduced him into an international fraternity of those like himself?" The twentieth-century book *Lesbian Nuns: Breaking Silence* documents the same experience of lesbians, some of whom enjoyed the relative safety of the convent over expectations to marry men.

But if we begin believing that the body is good, that all of our body parts are sacred, fashioned by God not only to warn us of pain but also for our pleasure and the pleasure of others, for our sexual union with a partner, for our spiritual communion with a community, and for our services of justice and charity on this earth—we have a glimpse of what the Creation and the Incarnation and the Resurrection are all about, signifying body and earth as glories of God and loci of God's presence in the world worthy of eternity. Even John "Total Depravity" Calvin declared, "Satan dazzles us . . . to imagine that we are polluted by intercourse."[21]

Body and earth positivity were the tenor of Celtic Christianity first discussed in Chapter Four. Writing in the fourth century, the Celtic writer Pelagius emphasized that creation and humanity were essentially good. "Pelagius maintained that the image of God can be seen in every newborn child and that, although obscured by sin, it exists at the heart of every person, waiting to be released through the grace of God," writes Church of Scotland minister J. Philip Newell in *Listening for the Heartbeat of God: A Celtic Spirituality*.[22] This directly contradicted Augustine of Hippo's notion that every child was born in sin, and that only the church and its sacraments may restore a person's *imago dei*. In the ninth century, John Scotus Eriugena (which simply means "John the Irishman from Ireland") affirmed that "Christ moves among us in two shoes, as it were, one shoe being that of creation, the other that of the Scriptures."[23]

And within this exalted view of humankind, Pelagius made one of the earliest references to what later became common practice in Celtic Christianity, the finding of a "soul friend," an *anamchara*, with whom, as Aelred of Riveaulx wrote to Bernard in *Mirror of Love* quoted earlier, "you can pour out your soul." A friend like this was considered of greater value than the church for spiritual guidance and self-discovery. This developed into what became known as the sacrament of confession and subsequently the rite of reconciliation in the Roman Catholic Church and morphed into the pastoral counseling movement among Protestants, a movement comprehensively documented in Anglican priest Kenneth Leech's book, *Soul Friend: The Practice of Christian Spirituality*. In recent years the soul-friend movement has gained ascendancy in the increasing numbers of spiritual directors within both Protestant and Catholic circles.

A husband often needs male friends who understand and challenge and support him in a way a wife cannot. A wife often needs female friends who understand and challenge and support her in a way a husband cannot. The blessing of same-gender partners is that at once they have a spouse and a same-gender friend. Thus there is at least the possibility of a deeper and more intense marriage than otherwise might be possible, an opportunity for partners, as Jonathan with David, to experience their souls knit together and to love the partner as "my own soul," to be soul-friends or soul-mates.

Of course it could be said that males with males and females with females do not enjoy the moderating influence of the opposite gender. First I would say even "gender" may be taken too literally, something to which all of us who do not fit our gender expectations can attest, whether liberated female or liberated male, whether lesbian, gay, bisexual, or transgender. Partners in same-gender relationships often find traditional masculine-feminine complentarity in their collective attributes. But the notion of "traditional" masculine-feminine characteristics also needs to be questioned.

The cultural permission and even encouragement of males to spread their seed prolifically and indiscriminately, perhaps rooted in biology, would be unchecked in male-male relationships, some might argue. The cultural expectation of females to focus on hearth and home is a necessary moderating influence in marriage, these might say. By this standard, lesbian relationships would meet the highest standard of marital "success." And the argument fails to note that marriage itself was understood as the answer to male "generosity." And now, in a time when women are freer to express themselves sexually because of birth control and evolving societal expectations, such distinctions between genders are less evident.

If marriage is viewed as a sacrament, the partners serve as "ministers of the sacrament" requiring no prerequisites of training or purity, a holy order alongside others that confers sanctification and grace. As a social estate, Luther nonetheless calls marriage "a divine and holy estate of life," a "blessed holy calling," and "church of God" that was to take in and care for strangers much as monasteries and cloisters.[24] As a covenant, Calvin claimed marriage as a vocation equal to all religious vocations, sanctifying what formerly was considered "dirty," containing a holiness closer to the reign of God than a cloister.[25] And as a commonwealth, marriage was considered a little church, "a kind of paradise on earth" that served as "seminary of the Church and the Commonwealth." [26] *The Kings Book* of 1543 placed "mutual aid and comfort" of marriage partners above procreation, and the 1559 Book of Common Prayer encouraged partners in marriage to be of "one accord of heart and mind" welcoming "pleasant and sweet love."[27]

Most readers would have little argument with any of these lofty considerations of marriage, though those who have experienced marriage firsthand may harbor doubts. What I have personally come to believe is that we might best view marriage as a little monastery, a contemplative order of the partners in marriage themselves, who have reined in conflicting desires in order to focus on one another (and their children, if so blessed) to love and honor and in some sense obey, obey as in mutually trusting one another's spiritual leadership. Taking marital vows could be ritualized by Jonathan's giving up his armor and weapons to David, letting go of our defenses and offenses to embrace the partner. Taking marital vows could be verbalized in Ruth's words to Naomi, "Where you go, I will go, your people shall be my people, your God my God."

And our "marital monasteries" may be of one heart, one mind, and one soul as the first Christian community was, sharing everything with one another and giving generously to those in need. John Boswell once said that one of the special graces of a gay household is its ready welcome of others needing a place to stay, to talk, to be comforted and cared for. Surely the compassionate response of the LGBT community to those living with HIV and AIDS, even as government and church lagged far behind, is evidence of the hospitality of Christ himself. And the community's advocacy for justice on their behalf is the political form of hospitality. This hospitality parallels that of those practiced by monastic orders that follow the Benedictine rule. This hospitality recalls that of the childless Sarah and Abraham, who thus entertained angels and Yahweh unaware. This hospitality was granted to religious outcasts by Jesus himself. This is the hospitality that the church is called to practice toward lesbian, gay, bisexual, and transgender people and same-gender marriages.

Summing up the spirituality and hospitality of the first Christian monastics, Thomas Merton wrote: "Love in fact *is* the spiritual life, and without it all the other exercises of the spirit, however lofty, are emptied of content and become mere illusions. The more lofty they are, the more dangerous the illusion."[28] Thus we need "a faith unconfounded, and a love without pretense" once honored in Christian liturgies solemnizing same-gender marriages. That's the blessing of marriage, to love another as one's own soul.

Notes

[1] Glaser, *Come Home!*, 191–192.

[2] *The New Oxford Annotated Bible with the Apocrypha, New Revised Standard Version* (New York: Oxford University Press, 1991), 854, annotation on Song of Solomon 1.1.

[3] Glaser, *Uncommon Calling*, 47–48.

[4] Tom Horner, *Jonathan Loved David* (Philadelphia: Westminster Press, 1976).

[5] Witte, *From Sacrament to Contract*, 20.

[6] Witte, 24.

[7] Witte, 26.

[8] Witte, 27.

[9] Witte, 28.

[10] Witte, 48.

[11] NBC Nightly News, December 29, 2008.

[12] Witte, *From Sacrament to Contract*, 48–53.

[13] Witte, 95.

[14] Witte, 98.

[15] Witte, 111–112.

[16] Witte, 174.

[17] Witte, 172.

[18] Daniel Rogers, *Matrimoniall Honour* (London: Philip Nevel, 1642), quoted in Witte, *From Sacrament to Contract*, 172.

[19] Witte, 197.

[20] Lisa Miller, "Our Mutual Joy," *Newsweek* (December 2008), *www.newsweek.com* (accessed March 27, 2009).

[21] From Calvin's sermon on Deuteronomy 5:18, quoted by Witte, *From Sacrament to Contract*, 107.

[22] Newell, *Listening for the Heartbeat of God*, 5–6.

[23] Newell, 34.

[24] Witte, *From Sacrament to Contract*, 49.

[25] Calvin's commentary on Genesis 2:18 quoted in Witte, *From Sacrament to Contract*, 110.

[26] Witte, *From Sacrament to Contract*, 171.

[27] Witte, 173.

[28] Thomas Merton, *The Wisdom of the Desert* (New York: New Directions Books, 1960), 17.